A BLACK MILLENNIAL
WOMAN IN PROGRESS

FAR AWAY

from

CLOSE

to

HOME

—— essays ——

VANESSA BADEN KELLY

THREE ROOMS PRESS
New York, NY

Far Away from Close to Home:
A Black Millennial Woman in Progress—essays
by Vanessa Baden Kelly

ISBN 978-1-953103-02-4 (trade paperback original)
ISBN 978-1-953103-03-1 (Epub)
Library of Congress Control Number: 2020949807

TRP-087

First Edition

Publication Date: May 4, 2021

BISAC category code
BIO002010 BIOGRAPHY & AUTOBIOGRAPHY / Cultural, Ethnic & Regional /
    African American & Black
SOC001000 SOCIAL SCIENCE / Ethnic Studies / American /African American Studies
LCO010000 LITERARY COLLECTIONS / Essays
LCO002010 LITERARY COLLECTIONS / American / African American

FRONT COVER DESIGN:
Victoria Black, www.thevictoriablack.com

BACK COVER ILLUSTRATION:
Barbara Friedman, www.barbarafriedmanpaintings.com

INTERIOR DESIGN:
KG Design International, www.katgeorges.com

DISTRIBUTED BY:
PGW/Ingram: www.pgw.com

Three Rooms Press
New York, NY
www.threeroomspress.com
info@threeroomspress.com

FAR AWAY

from

CLOSE

to

HOME

*For my Grandmother and Joanna DiPeppe—
who have encouraged me to write my thoughts
as long as I've been writing.*

*For Ryder—everything I do is dedicated to you.
Mommy loves you as big as God's underwear.*

TABLE OF CONTENTS

FAR AWAY
from
CLOSE
to
HOME

« ONE »

STOP

The smell is the first thing that hit me. It wasn't the smell of exhaust or rubber or whatever other material is used on a Los Angeles city bus. It was distinct. A stench we somehow all know but cannot identify how we know it. Like blood or death. The smell was human. Unbathed. Urinated. Downtrodden. Somewhere on that bus, a human person reeked of both living and slowly dying. Not the long-day-of-work smell. Or the just-leaving-the-gym smell. But the stench of days on a street. No running water. Perhaps no water to drink. I had grown accustomed to this smell from walking east on Sunset Boulevard. Past the Walk of Fame on Vine Street. Past the huge billboards and building long advertisements for multi-million-dollar films and too expensive coffee. Past $5,000/month condos and cafes with pet parking. Past all of that. But not *too* far past. Just a few blocks east, to the corner of Gower where the same stench that was on that bus fills the air, thick, in the same way a nose is assaulted by more pleasant odors in a city: bacon wrapped hot dogs or new air fresheners in an Uber. This was the smell of a person looking for a home.

It didn't take me long to find the source. Instinctively, I walked all the way to the back of the bus to sit down. I could hear my childhood teachers scolding me in my head: "We fought too long and too hard for any Black person to choose the back of the bus." I heard their arguments and I respected their position, but the convenience of not being bumped every time someone had to get off the bus gave me reason to believe that, instead, my ancestors had fought for my choice to sit where I wanted, and today I was choosing the back. I sauntered through the bus, nodding at the bus driver, quietly hoping for an easy, no-human-interaction ride into Hollywood. My ride to work, which was normally thirty to forty minutes, would now take over an hour on public transportation. I would have to creep through neighborhoods and side streets that I would love to live in but could not afford, as gentrification prices of middle-class Los Angeles communities of color rose higher and higher. Of course, without gentrification, I would have hated to live there, and that was a reality I struggled with daily. I would also be crossing through neighborhoods not yet gentrified but well on their way. Ones that I would be happy to be in the back for, to avoid the seemingly unsavory (whatever that meant), the people who could tell I don't normally take the bus, the people Los Angeles allows you to forget about in your tiny enclave of security.

I hadn't ridden the bus beyond airport transfers and major events since 2012. Back then, I had accumulated too many parking tickets in my car, and the city had impounded it. Because I did not yet have a California driver's license, due to the fact that I did not yet have a permanent address, I couldn't make payments on the tickets to get my car back. Instead, I would have to pay the bulk of them up front. In an elaborately bureaucratic showcase of how expensive it is to be poor in America, I would lose my car. Of course I didn't have the money to pay the parking tickets up front. If I had, I could've paid the tickets when they were received. Or fed myself. Every day my car stayed impounded it rose in cost for the "storage fee" at the city lot. *Two hundred fifty dollars every day* dollars a day. After rallying for the payments, I eventually let my car go. I went to the lot to pull anything valuable out of the car. A few plaid T-shirts. Notebooks. A pair of shoes. I left my skateboard in the trunk. I didn't think I would have time to skate anymore. In a city where it's so expensive to be jobless, I couldn't imagine having time to enjoy life. Skateboarding in LA had become the pastime of those rich enough to have extra time, masquerading themselves as those too carefree and "of the city" to care that they were identified with "alt" culture. Los Angeles has a way of even gentrifying survival. I didn't want to be a part of any of it. The amount of bus riding that I did in between losing my first car and buying my next made me avoid the massive orange tankers even while driving. It reminded me of harder times.

But here I was today, taking a line into work that I otherwise would have avoided if not specifically asked by a friend to do so. To "experience the city" again. My headphones slid from the inside of my hoodie to my ears as I walked further through the bus. No music was coming through the buds. A trick learned in the city was that headphones in ears was the universal sign for "don't fuck with me, don't speak to me, don't breathe in my general direction." It was a respected sign. One being employed throughout this bus. The brunette in the ill-fitting red suit and New Balance sneakers was holding a sign. The young Black barista, in his Starbucks apron, was holding his as well. He made me think of coffee.

"I should get some when I get to Hollywood," I thought. I caught eyes and gave a head nod to the older Black woman sitting towards the middle, leaning her reusable shopping bag against the accordion that allowed the bus to stretch, much like the city had, beyond capacity. I could've ignored her. She understood my sign. But I felt respect was due someone her age, still having to lug her bags and her life across a bustling city on public transportation. She was probably in her late 60s.

"Where are her children?" I wondered. "Why are they allowing her to ride the bus at her age?"

I immediately wondered why I supposed she had children. Perhaps because she looked like someone I knew. Not anyone in particular. Just someone. She wore compression socks and orthopedic shoes that told a story of a woman who had long left walking behind. It wouldn't matter anyway. Nothing in this part of the city had the coveted "high walk score" that rental websites boasted about. The more necessities (and luxuries) that a person can walk to in Los Angeles makes the area more desirable for renters. It also raises the price. Which makes no sense, because if you can pay those prices, you probably own a car. Paradoxes. The greater paradox, of course, is that the richer people in LA seemed to be, the more they coveted the ability to walk everywhere. Teslas in their driveways as they walked to the local farmer's market. I suppose it was a novelty.

I wondered where she lived and how far she'd have to carry this bag when she did get off the bus. Someone should help her. Not me of course. I had to get to work. I knew that was shitty. But so was this whole city.

Los Angeles has been the best and worst place I've ever lived. It is the city I adore. My forever home. The place I refuse to leave because I could never imagine raising my son anywhere else. So much so that I have agonized over where we live within the city. Angelenos rep the district where they were raised with pride. I love the idea of him boasting the Crenshaw district or saying he grew up in Eagle Rock. I wouldn't mind Pasadena—it's no LA but close enough that Angelenos hold a common respect, and it's still in Los Angeles County. But the idea of him repping overly gentrified areas like Silver Lake or West Adams rubs me wrong. An outsider's point of view, because many Angelenos grew up in those areas before the gentrification began, many still remain and are proud. I love that my family—especially my son—will have that pride. Home ownership, even if we always rent. Los Angeles is full of cultural and business opportunity and some of the best neighborhoods and neighbors I have ever experienced. It's also a place with so much opportunity spoiled by poor economics, poor leadership, and a general malaise in trying to find ways to fix it.

I moved to Los Angeles from Florida in 2010. For a young person looking to find something, LA will have it. Even if they don't yet know what that something is. Every scene, every culture, every taste, every brand is represented in the city. But they aren't all represented together. What I quickly found is that life felt far more segregated in Los Angeles County than it ever felt in Florida. When I first came to LA, I lived in Montecito Heights, an area of northeast LA with views of downtown, on a street that touched both Cypress Park and Chinatown. In that time, I could count how many Black people I saw. Racist redlining practices had long ago segregated the city. There were some areas that Black folks from LA would never go, even with many of those restrictions pretending to be gone. Pretending being the operative word. Transplants like myself and others didn't know any better.

I never saw white people in Montecito Heights either. Not then anyway. Only Mexican, Nicaraguan, and Honduran. Chinese if I went far enough down the street. Where I lived in Montecito Heights was a walkable area because so few people had cars, but the brown skin that filled most homes and apartments had helped it to escape the capitalistic claws of yuppies. Hipsters, the neo-yuppie with an affinity for brown areas like Montecito Heights for the sake of "urban authenticity" but a privileged fear of the schools and parks and people that make urban areas "authentic," were just beginning to move in. I lived close to Lincoln Park—some would argue I should say I lived in Lincoln Park, but El Sereno residents would disagree—so it was more bustling than the "Wilderness In The City" motto Wikipedia alleges residents refer to it as. I never heard a single person say that. I did hear Lincoln Park though. There were at least three supermarkets within a mile. Restaurants. Clothing stores. Lawyers. Dentists. Reception halls. All of those things on one main street—not ironically called Main Street—that could be popped in and out of on any given day. Signs were in

Spanish. Everything was painted. No flashy LED lights or custom-made signs like Hollywood.

Everything felt brown. Not just the people but the buildings. Even trees in full bloom in the spring somehow felt like brick or that special shade of brown that Weimaraners are. But there were no Weimaraners here. Just pit bulls and chihuahuas. The occasional indiscriminate fluffy dog. Buildings all seemed dingy although older Spanish-speaking women could be seen sweeping and hosing down sidewalks every day, chatting and laughing with each other from across the street. I stuck out but never felt unsafe. The area was central to two major freeways and there was a train station next door to the building where I was staying with longtime friends of my family. They lived in a fairly new condo, selling at low prices for the city, high prices for the area, in hopes of attracting young white families. They were trickling in. Beneath the overpass of one of those free-ways was a little squatter settlement. One settler had a bed frame, a vanity, and a dining room table. Every few weeks, LAPD would move them all from under the overpass and the table would be gone. Within days, it would be back. Under that overpass was the squatter's home. Loitering was only illegal when people complained. Because people of color don't tend to call the police on each other, it was easy to determine who kept reporting the settlement. My building.

When I moved to North Hollywood two years later, it was my very first apartment with *my* name on it. I moved there because I was attending a church that I loved and that served as a hub for young, up-and-coming artists of color. I saw a few more Black people. But I knew them all. Or at least would come to know them. That area was the transplant hub of LA. It had (and still has) extremely reasonable rent (as far as big cities go) but still offers a place worth living in without too much of a commute or worries about safety. It looked kind of nice, depending where you were. Greener. Young and vibrant, not in infrastructure but in what the young folks call "vibe." The neighborhood knew it was a place artists were flocking to and created the "Arts District," a moderately walkable area in the southernmost part of North Hollywood. There were bars and ramen restaurants. Places for live music were installed, surrounding already-existing rehearsal studios and dance schools. It seemed like the Hollywood dream to anyone new. I met my husband there. We dated there. We got married living there. It seemed like young love blossomed in this part of Los Angeles. So many young people dreaming about and creating the future they moved here to find.

I remember when I got married the first thing everyone said was "Where are you all going to move to?" It was understood that married people don't *really* belong in North Hollywood. That was for newbies and the unsettled. Of course, married people *had* to live there. There are decent schools and many, many single-family homes with manicured lawns and signs that say things like "Drive like your kid is playing on this street." I don't know who those families are. My guess was always the white people. NoHo had them. They were unassuming and completely unmoved by the artist community in their residential areas and neighborhood Ralph's, where dancers could sometimes be seen miming yesterday's choreography in the cereal aisle. All of the young North Hollywood transplants hung out at the same places. At that time, most of us went to the same church. Those that didn't fuck with Jesus knew someone at that church. There was only a degree of separation between you and any person of color in North Hollywood. In that way it felt safe. And like a small town in the middle of a metropolis.

No one in the North Hollywood artistic community really ever had to leave North Hollywood when their careers were on the rise. However, the moment a career began to take off and a singer or a dancer or actress started budding and needed to do shows or visit studios, the majority of their time would need to be spent in the city of LA. The *city* of Los Angeles, right over the hills in a land two to three times the rent of the San Fernando Valley, with much faster walkers and exponentially worse traffic, represented opportunities that many in NoHo were still fighting to get and still seemed foreign. There was affordable housing—sort of—in LA proper, but it was dark and dingy and tight like Montecito Heights. Entering the "real" Los Angeles somehow felt like entering into an abyss. One that everyone dreamed of but was also terrifying: becoming a true Angeleno. Sometimes it felt like people pretended to never want to leave North Hollywood so they would never have to try to survive over the hill. Living in the valley was hard enough. Expensive. Hundreds, if not thousands, of miles away from home for many. But still manageable. You could still say "I live in LA" without the actual scary realities of living in a metropolis. Marriage made us have to consider a move into the city. Both of our careers were moving rapidly, and we spent a great deal of time in LA. We thought about staying in North Hollywood. Moving near the white people who occupied so many of the residential neighborhoods, but it didn't feel like the NoHo we had come to know. Being there felt like a displacement, new and far from the art community. If we were going to feel displaced, we decided, we would choose to be displaced to an area where more people looked like us. Many of the people on that bus probably could have benefited from North Hollywood prices. But like us, there was a good chance they braved higher rent and smaller square footage, poor walk scores, and public transportation to live in a community that felt like home.

North Hollywood truly was home to some ethnic groups. There is a tale of two cities in every major city in the US. There is the city the transplants, like me, see. And the version the natives and those who have lived there long enough to raise children come to know. North of Burbank Boulevard was the real NoHo. Past the newly contrived Arts District and new developments. The San Fernando Valley—or the Valley—was created for below-line workers in the entertainment industry. An affordable option for mostly white families who couldn't afford to live in Beverly Hills. Like Leimert Park and Country Club Estates in the more southern parts of Los Angeles County (but in the city of LA), and various other areas below the Interstate 10, integration and the low cost of living attracted other races. White people fled. Many single-family homes were replaced with multifamily homes, and a once white enclave became a mostly Latino immigrant-populated city with pockets of white homeowners. The new brown faces changed the attitude toward the Valley. The well-to-do never looked highly on it—it was working class after all—but as time progressed it was considered a cultural wasteland. White folks did what white folks do and tried to separate the "us" and "thems." Valley Village. The Arts District. Whatever they could. Those places are evidence of what Mayor Eric Garcetti vowed to "clean up," along with South Central Los Angeles, in his campaign for mayor. North Hollywood got browner and browner as one would travel north of Burbank Boulevard.

The apartment I first moved into was south of Burbank Boulevard. Everyone I was around was an artist. We didn't know any other part of NoHo. Everything we could ever need was south. I moved in with my boyfriend (who would later become my husband) in 2013. He and his roommate lived far north in the Valley. An area of NoHo that bordered Sunland. It truly only depended where you stepped if you were in either North Hollywood or someplace else. When I moved in, a mere two miles north of my old North Hollywood apartment, I realized how little I had seen of the place I claimed to live. On Día De Los Muertos, Day of the Dead, a huge skeleton Virgin Mary was erected in the front yard behind our apartment building. When we came back home that day, it seemed half of the Sunland population had stopped by to leave flowers, unopened bottles of liquor, and cash. Every Sunday, the speakers from a local iglesia flooded our room. The sidewalk was cluttered with hundreds of people attending the Protestant church service but who couldn't fit inside the storefront church. Women holding the hands of Mary-Jane-and-bobby-socked little girls, older Latino men in western regalia down to the cowboy boots and hats, elderly couples in walkers that double as seats sat on that sidewalk. So the church projected the service. As pedestrians passed they would make the sign of the cross. Not necessary for non-Catholic services, but they respected the sidewalk clergy. The Spanish-speaking pastor's voice became our alarm clock. It was 9:00 a.m. Every other day of the week we didn't have to worry about an alarm clock either. Someone had a rooster that cock-a-doodled at precisely 8:45 a.m. I guess he respected the sidewalk clergy as well. He never clucked on Sunday. Until that point, Los Angeles had only been white and brown.

* * *

THIS BUS WAS VERY BLACK AND white, something I found odd. I expected more young people of all races, I guess. They seemed to have more mobility in the city. Transplants of any race had no loyalty to the enclaves of Los Angeles. They went where they could find a place to live. Couch surfing or otherwise. The woman with her bag resting against the accordion, though, was curious. The bus from Glendale into Hollywood went through Glendale to Atwater Village,

Atwater to Silver Lake. Because the bus routes make such little sense, instead of continuing east to Hollywood, the bus veers south to Rampart Village, clips Koreatown, then comes back into Hollywood. To keep going straight east, you'd have to transfer. Public transportation in LA is shoddy at best and the only way you can guarantee to get to your destination on time is to stay your ass on the bus and go the long way. None of the stops had Black people. None like the woman in the middle of the bus at least. "People like her" were in South LA, Inglewood, Compton, and further south. There was a thriving

Black community in Pasadena, but Pasadena folks didn't come down to the city much. Especially not on the bus. From where I lived in Glendale, the bus was a haul. I was only on it today because I was told to "see the city through a different lens" by a mentor. I accepted the challenge. But the length of the ride and stench of the riders made me regret the decision.

The long row of blue seats against the back of the bus were hard and musty. Someone was already looking out of the window on the left, so I sat on the other end to lean against the window on the right. There were still plenty of seats. The gentrification in Atwater and Silver Lake made bus riding easy in those areas. People were "too climate conscious" to ride a gas-guzzling bus. Instead, all two million gentrifiers drove individual low-emission vehicles. Mostly Priuses. That made sense to them. Once we got into Rampart Village, the bus would fill. I was lucky to get on when I did. The homeless man, whose stench was crowding what physical bodies weren't, was a few rows ahead of me. Slouched in an entire row. Asleep against the window. He was a person of color. I would've guessed Black, but frankly, it was hard to tell. He was so dirty and blackened by streets and corrupt homelessness policies of the city it was hard to tell his ethnicity. A few years earlier the city had replaced every bus stop bench with benches that had dividers. They said it was for more individual seating to encourage folks to ride the bus. It was really to discourage homeless people from sleeping on those benches. I took the homeless man's riding of the bus as an act of defiance. A middle finger to the city. If they won't let you sleep on the bus bench, collect $1.50 and sleep on the fucking bus.

He probably wasn't thinking that at all. It was hot. Far hotter than it should have been in late September. The week had seen temperatures upwards of the nineties. Where the asphalt was black, it felt even hotter. The squiggly lines of desert heat rising from the concrete were visible from windows. Walking to your car felt as though you were testing fate. Or evaporation. Sleeping, let alone living on pavement must have been excruciating. I could have picked up my smartphone and complained about his presence. I could've marched right back to the bus driver and asked her to get him off. Anyone on the bus could have. None of us did. Maybe some were used to it. There was a deep sense, however, that everyone was thinking what I was thinking: this smell sucks, but he can't go back out there. It's too damn hot.

Downtown LA had long been the hub of the city's homeless residents. All of the nonprofit organizations, shelters, and ministries that serve the homeless are concentrated in a small section, a few blocks long and a couple of blocks wide, that the upper crust of LA call Skid Row. People from the area called it the Nickel because it takes up a large portion of Fifth Street. The Nickel is directly adjacent to the Downtown Arts District. One side of Alameda Street is littered with garbage and needles and tents. The other side has chic coffee bars and murals of things like Frida Kahlo or a butterfly with the center open so you can take a selfie with wings. One side booms obscenities and sirens. On the other, Ed Sheeran is playing quietly. There seems to be a new documentary about one side of Alameda Street every other year. That documentary will send people on the other side of Alameda Street into an outrage as it ends on

Netflix and they discuss it over pad thai. The next day, they'll get into their Prius, cross over Alameda through the Nickel, and barely give people in the tents a passing glance. There are approximately ten thousand homeless people at any given time in Downtown LA. They are like landmarks. You know they are there, but they are part of the landscape. You learn to see through them. As though they weren't people. Rather an unfortunate price to pay for exposed brick and reclaimed warehouse live/work spaces.

The man on the bus didn't look like someone from Skid Row. The resources the homeless have in the Nickel from all of the organizations around them make them a different "type" of homeless, if there ever was such a thing. (A presumption that is based on no facts and fills me with shame that I even believe there to be a "type" of homeless.) He was despondent. Smelly. Dirty. Exhausted. A good indicator that he may be mentally ill or have a drug addiction. Unable to stay sane or clean long enough to stay in a community of other homeless, he was a lone wolf. Which meant he may be erratic. A light bulb went off in my head: he's still on the bus because no one wants to upset him. They don't know what he will do. I pulled my bag a little closer. Watching from my peripheral for the rest of the ride. I took out my phone and texted my husband.

"Damnit. I'm stuck behind a homeless guy."

"In Silver Lake?! Is he cool?"

"He's asleep."

"Cool enough. Keep your head on a swivel. Is he Black?"

"I think."

"He'll be cool."

We'd done this a million times in a million different places. Just never in these parts of town. One thing we knew is that Black homeless people, unless deeply mentally disturbed, left us alone.

* * *

AFTER WE GOT MARRIED AND LEFT North Hollywood, we moved to South LA. All the Black people we had missed in the rest of the city, we found there. I worked for a large community organizing NPO at the time, the same one that had put out fires physically and within the community of the '92 riots. The non-profit often touted that Los Angeles had the highest population of black people in America only second to Kings County. Only Brooklyn outdid us. Had I heard that statistic before moving to South LA, I would have laughed. Before South LA, church was the most Black people I had seen in one place. But South LA, not the one of the movies or nightly news, was a gem. It *is* a gem. South LA made us Angelenos. We considered ourselves California residents as a result of living there. It made us part of the community, it made us engage in city politics. It made us proud of our block. We lived on Seventy-Eighth and Crenshaw. The Blackest you could get in the city. Everything was Black. Doctors. Dentists. Teachers. Lawyers. Bankers. Homeless. Homeowners. If there was an adjective to describe the Crenshaw District, it was Black. And it included all swaths of life. From the troubled Westmont District to the "Black Beverly Hills," Ladera Heights. Neither my husband nor I had ever seen anything like it.

We rented a three-bedroom Spanish home in Park Mesa Heights. Everyone around us was a homeowner. We had block parties. A year into living there, I got pregnant. My neighbors dropped by with things they had picked up at the store. They sent food when my husband was working. When my dog got out they returned her, knowing exactly who she belonged to. Everyone was working- to middle class. In the two years we lived there, LA got zoned to have two more sports teams and got the bid for the Olympics, both of which would be housed about a mile away. That year, a house on our street that was sold for $250,000 a year prior was sold for $500,000, and someone saw a white girl jogging down Crenshaw. The early signs of gentrification were there. But it hadn't ruined us yet. When my son was born, his first day care was two houses down at a home care on my street. And I had choices. The house on the end of the block was also a home care center. I chose the one closer because the woman at the end had a glass eye. I was a new mom and worried her vision would impair her ability. No one else did. Her center had a waiting list. She was only making an exception for me because I was a neighbor.

In the house directly across the street from us was an old woman whose name we could never remember. She sat on her porch all day long. My husband would take out the garbage and she would yell to him to pick up his pants. One day she asked him to come over. He obliged.

"Why you wear your pants so low?"

"It's stylish."

"To who?"

"I will pick them up."

"They gonna think you wanna them boys. You're not. You have a wife and a family that needs you. Keep yourself together."

They, of course, were the LAPD. Those boys were the boys next door to her. Directly to the west of her was a vacant home. The occupant had died before we ever moved in. But the home was still in the family. No one lived there for real, but the grandson of the deceased was there frequently. "Banging," as they called it. The whole block hated it. A communal block of older families and elderly had this one sore spot. We assumed they were selling drugs because there would be the occasional straggler who no one knew, and late at night, cars would be parked out front that didn't belong to anyone on the street. That's where we learned that even Black addicts didn't mess with Black people if you stayed cool. Even in a crack-induced haze, we had a quiet understanding that we left each other alone. We were all just trying to make it.

In the house to the west of the vacant house was an older woman and her adult daughter Keisha. Keisha sold drugs. But she sold them in the city. She didn't believe in selling drugs in her own neighborhood. And she didn't sell hard stuff. Just weed, sometimes pills, to people in the gentrifying West Adams. Since weed was legal, now her clientele had dropped. But there were still a lot of people who wanted what she had, either because they didn't want a record of their consumption or POs wouldn't allow it. Keisha was my favorite part of our block. She was the watchdog, the community police, and the Aunt of everyone she met. She helped me bring in all the baby furniture that was delivered and walked with me around the block at night to help "walk the baby down." When my grandmother arrived three weeks before I gave birth, she'd watch us walk from the porch and talk about my progress. I remember waving at her and her blowing me a kiss as we drove away the night I went into labor. She rarely wore a bra. Her hair was always a mess. She had dark cocoa skin and you could barely see the white of her eyes. She was wonderful.

I had my eyes set on a specific couch when we moved into the South LA house, and as I waited for it to go on sale, we rented furniture. When it finally hit the price point I wanted, we bought it, put the rental couch on the porch, and told the company we rented from to come pick it up. We left the gate to our porch unlocked while we ran a few errands. As we were on our way home, we received a frantic call from the pickup driver. A crazed woman was trying to assault him and prevent him from picking up the couch. We could hear Keisha's voice, shrilly screaming "fuck you, cracka" in the phone. We yelled to try to get her attention, but she didn't listen. When we arrived, the delivery men were locked in their truck. Keisha in front of our porch. We explained the situation. She thought they were repossessing our furniture.

"You all gotta tell me when shit like this is happening. No one's house gets fucked with on this street."

The delivery drivers wouldn't make eye contact with her. She beat their window.

"Don't act like you don't hear me, muthafuckas." And she walked home. We were so grateful for her patrol we bought her a bottle of expensive vodka that night. She requested that same bottle for her birthday and Christmas. We got a bigger one each time.

Keisha often fought the boys next door. Physically fought them. With belts or brooms or bats. She hated them destroying the street and not being respectful of the neighborhood. Keisha didn't bang, but everyone who did respected her and understood how she felt. So the boys had to listen to her. If they were parked too close to our driveway, they knew to move their cars when one of us walked out. When we came outside with our son, they went inside, leaving only the faintest smell of weed to remind anyone that they were there. But they still caused trouble. Police were there far more often as the years went on. Eventually there was a raid on the house. Five young Black men were handcuffed, face-down on our front lawn. One was kicked. My husband witnessed all of it from inside with our son.

He called me at work. "We have to leave the neighborhood."

"Why?"

"Ryder can't see our people like this."

* * *

A FEW MONTHS LATER, WE WERE in Glendale. We never saw Black people again. Not like that anyway. We have mourned it since we left and vowed if we could ever price back into the more affluent neighborhoods of South LA, we would go back. But we valued Ryder's sense of self too much to let a fucked-up system ruin his idea of who and what he is before he ever has a chance. Now, the struggle is stopping the preconceived notions of those areas become his reality. It feels hopeless sometimes. Like the only thing we can do as parents is try our best to keep him alive and let God sort out the rest.

Glendale was a choice of convenience. It was central to our jobs. Clean and young and blossoming with home ownership possibilities. A huge outdoor shopping area with trolleys and fountains was a little over a decade old and kept money and population pouring into the area. In turn, the public schools were decent and only on the ascent. You could be anywhere in LA in about thirty minutes tops. It was a good choice. The demographic was largely white. But also largely Armenian. It was the hub for Armenian immigrants after the genocide. Historically, Glendale was the Ku Klux Klan capital of LA, and people of color had to be out by dark.

Armenians had pushed many of the overt racists further north. Those white people now had two areas of their own—the city of La Canada and an area of north Glendale called La Crescenta-Montrose. The latter two areas are still a part of the Glendale city systems but have their own government and a school district. They are areas with some of the best schools in the county. They are also some of the few pockets of conservative voting districts in all of Los Angeles. It has been nice. It has been as close to Mayberry as LA can get. It's still no South LA.

The bus came to a stop in Hollywood. Surprisingly, it hadn't filled much more after Rampart Village. There were more people than before but still plenty of seats open, and no one had messed with the homeless man at all. My stop was the next one. I could have gotten off closer to my job, but I wanted to grab some coffee first. Five-dollar cups that years ago I wouldn't have dared waste my money on. I pulled the yellow rubber string that indicated I needed to get off. I made my way to the front before the bus hydraulics slowly broke the bus to a stop. I wanted to get off fast. The smell was tolerable, but barely. As I passed back by the homeless man I tried to inconspicuously look at his face. He was Black. I said a silent prayer: "Jesus, help him with whatever he needs help with." A rush of guilt followed. Perhaps I was his help somehow. Perhaps someone on the bus was and we all were just leaving him alone and letting him sleep. As quickly as the guilt came it left, and I continued moving forward. Somehow I had missed the woman next to the accordion get off the bus. I wondered where she had gone. I could not think of one viable place a woman like her could have wanted to go in the places we stopped at. Perhaps she wasn't going anywhere she wanted to go. Perhaps she was going where she had to go. Just like the rest of us. Just like I was going to work from a place in Glendale I was more than happy to live in but never would have chosen. Or the homeless man in the back going nowhere, probably wishing to be going anywhere but the way he is. I felt myself thinking too deeply about people I would never see again, people that would drown in a sea of 22 million people in Los Angeles County.

My bus stop came and I walked off. I nodded at the driver. One last look at the homeless man in the back and all the riders whose faces did not reflect the stench he emitted.

"Tomorrow," I thought to myself, "I'll drive the Prius."

TWO

SYBRINA, GINA, AND ME

Everyone dabbed at their eyes as Robert Anderson stood behind a concrete support beam and wept loudly. He didn't bother to remove his gold-rimmed glasses as he hid his face, tears staining the same light blue dress shirt he had worn to every press conference since the ordeal began. He was tall and lanky, like his fourteen-year-old son Martin had been at the time of his death. In his youth, you could have easily mistaken him for a basketball player with his height and slender build, though his commitment to being clean-cut may have made him seem not quite "that type" of Black man. His now-deceased son's hair was in short dreadlocks that barely touched his shoulders. He was not mistaken for a basketball player. Instead, he was mistaken for a full-grown man.

There is something about seeing an otherwise stoic adult cry that elicits the deepest sadness . . . When I watched his father cry over a year later, I had empathy for him. His age was of no consequence. He was in pain. Martin had been too. Watching those tears was devastating to me.

His ex-wife, Gina Jones, who after months and months of press conferences barely ever broke down—not a tear or crack in her voice—wept as well. Perhaps it was seeing how emotional Robert had become. Perhaps it was because she was standing in front of five white faces arguing for her son's humanity. Faces that, like the rest of the world, had watched the final moments of her son Martin's life strangled to death by Bay County police officers. Now they were asking her to make a case for why the state should be held accountable. Martin's family was suing the State of Florida for the death of their son. Some thought it a money grab, a "welfare queen trying to rape the state." To them it was attempting to get some sort of justice in any way they could. Someone had to be held accountable. They said that through their tears. Every Black face in that room understood their sentiment. Every Black face in the room cried.

"You just see a little Black boy," Gina said, her words stronger than either she or Robert seemed physically. "But that there, that there is my baby. He isn't 'was' my baby. He IS my baby. And he gonna be my baby 'til I die."

Windows lined the otherwise all-white space and made it feel like more of a conference center than a hearing room at the State Capitol. Extra blue plastic chairs had been brought in for the dozens of people—activists, onlookers, press—all there to see how the white faces in front of Gina and Robert would rule. Maybe even just to see what folks would say. I looked out of the window. I didn't want to catch eyes with either of Martin's parents. I didn't want my tears to compound theirs. Palm trees swayed in the cool morning wind. It was Good Friday in a northerner's paradise. Sixty-nine degrees in

April. Tourists flocked for the warm weather and, like true Floridians, we were in long sleeved shirts. Not made for how "cold" it was. Tallahassee was situated at almost the northernmost part of Florida, so if it were to be cold anywhere it would be there. Legend had it that the city had once seen snow flurries. But not that year. It was too warm for snow. Just like the summer would be brutally hot. Hot. The heat matched the tempers of the state the summer of 2007. Everyone was what the South calls "thirty-eight hot." Mad. Angry. Frustrated. Those feelings were pointed at the Florida Department of Law Enforcement for killing Martin Lee Anderson less than two hours after he had arrived at Bay County Boot Camp. A place Gina Jones had brought her son for help keeping him on the straight and narrow. The people that were supposed to help him killed him.

The other side of the outrage was pointed at the raucous college students and Black legislators who marched, sat in, and raised hell in hellish heat to demand justice for her boy. Who made then-governor Jeb Bush come back early from a presidential-candidate-prep trip to Iraq. Who made then little-known Chicago Senator Barack Obama and his professor wife release statements and think pieces. Jesse Jackson came. Al Sharpton came. They were making Florida seem disgraceful and the distaste was high.

The winter weather would cool the air. Spring would crisp the air. Nothing would clear it.

I was one of the raucous college students many in the state had come to hate. I was twenty-one. A junior at Florida State. Always the shortest and likely the loudest. I had a brother thirteen years younger than I was. He was eight. I was born and raised as a Black woman in Florida and I had gone through the day my uncle came home crying to my grandmother that his middle school girlfriend had to break up with him because her father found out he was Black, the stories of my uncles ripping down confederate flags from fellow high school students' trucks. I sat through the racial tensions of schools: "Black jokes" from teachers and all the "you're not like them" from apologetic white friends who had overgeneralized a brother or a sister and labeled them in my presence, knowing it was wrong and offering amends, but unwilling to back down from their belief. When the case of Martin Lee Anderson came to the law firm for which I was a part-time receptionist, my college job no longer felt like a means to make sure I had enough money to eat. Instead, it became the means by which I could protect my brother. His sweet, slight, elementary-age body was all I could see when I saw lanky, cocoa-skinned Martin's body go limp at the hands of 6 guards. Watching him wheeled away in that grainy video, knowing now what they didn't know then—that he would never return—felt like a gut punch.

When state documents were uncovered by the *Miami Herald* and the cover up we all suspected came to light, that video became a clarion call: act now or it will be my brother next. Your brother. Your uncle. Your son.

The guards who killed Martin would all be acquitted. In a scene no one in that time will ever forget, one of the attorneys would come out smiling, telling *Court TV,* "Our coloreds here are law abiding. They were never mad. The coloreds from elsewhere just didn't understand." Gina and Robert would relocate from Panama City, unable to stay in the city that had killed their child without even a formal apology. But they would leave their baby there. Buried once, exhumed for the trial, and buried again, they didn't want to disturb him. They'd lost him twice.

The day we all cried with Gina and Robert in the court room resulted in them winning their case. It was the largest settlement in Florida history, two million dollars. The cacophony of people screaming that this was a "money grab" from a family who "raised a thug and just wants a pay day from our tax dollars" was ever present, and seemed to grow louder and louder in the days of the hearing. But those voices weren't in that courtroom. They didn't hear the pain of the parents. They weren't there for any of the intimate moments of the year we fought for justice for Martin Lee Anderson. They only knew what they saw in one-minute clips on the nightly news and what was discussed over coffee after fiery CNN commentator Nancy Grace would eviscerate the Florida Justice Department. And that was enough. What we saw, what I saw, was different. It was pain. It was commonality. It was words that would echo in every chamber of my heart for the rest of my life.

"He gonna be my baby 'til I die."

* * *

ALMOST A DECADE AFTER THE DEATH of Martin Lee Anderson, tiny chubby hands reached into my shirt. It was a texture thing. He liked skin. Every night he pinched his round little belly, belly button still protruding from a hernia formed when they clamped it at birth, until he fell asleep. When he was still an infant and we would rock him to sleep, he would pinch the soft skin of our necks. Two little tan fingers the size of twigs with razor sharp fingernails would tear you up. You wouldn't dare move. There was nothing scarier than the thought of impeding him actually going to sleep. I would quietly yelp as I watched his big brown eyes, ones my husband would call "little puddles of wonderful," grow lower and lower. I would wonder how I could love something so much that my heart would want to jump out of my chest, how I could love something so much I would allow them to draw blood for their comfort. We would laugh about it later. Look at it in fond remembrance, even. In the moment, it was beautiful agony.

In those moments it was impossible to not think of the mothers who had lost their children. What it felt like to look at their sons, the same way I was looking at mine, in their caskets. When your children are so young you look at their faces and wonder how they will mature. You wonder what they will be like. Who they will marry. How it will be to watch them explore the world the same way you did. I would often think, "When they were feeding their son, they didn't know what was coming." I'd hug mine a little tighter. Cry for him. And I'd cry for those mothers.

I thought of Gina often. I thought more often of Sybrina Fulton, Trayvon Martin's mother. The thought wasn't random. Six years after Martin Lee Anderson's death, after my graduations and cross-country moves, Trayvon Martin was killed in Sanford by a man who used Stand Your Ground as a defense for profiling a Black teen. The world was on fire. Trayvon's name became iconic. He was 17.

By 2012, I had moved to Los Angeles. I had spent several years community organizing after Martin Lee Anderson. I realized that what we always needed was press—we needed the media to care and pick up the story—and had switched my course to Hollywood. I still organized within the arts for a local nonprofit, but I was nowhere protesting anymore.

I found out about Trayvon's death early. Not because his parents had chosen the same law firm I worked at that had handled the Martin Lee Anderson case (which Trayvon's parents chose for that reason), but because my grandparents lived in Central Florida. I was born and raised there. That's where my brother was. The local newspaper had run the story in the days following Trayvon's murder. Weeks before the nation would find out that a teenager had been gunned down for carrying Skittles and an Arizona iced tea. I remember my Republican, NRA card-carrying Grandpa telling me it sounded like "some coward picked a fight with a kid and lost, so he shot him." He then told me Benjamin Crump was listed as the family attorney.

I called Ben Crump that day. Both he and his law partner Daryl Parks had been like surrogate fathers to me when I started working at their firm. That had not changed since I moved. As soon as he picked up the phone he said, "You heard what's going on here?"

"Yeah I did. What really happened?"

"It's bad, baby."

"Can you win this?"

Pause.

"We're going to try. It seems too clear not to win. But you remember Martin."

Of course I did. And Ben did, too. Months after Martin Lee Anderson's case was over, when I was locking up for the night, I would sometimes find Ben in his office. Laptop open. Familiar scenes of that grainy video of Martin being beaten. If you asked him why he was watching it, his response was always the same: motivation to keep fighting.

I called my mother that night. She was livid. Ever the liberal in a staunchly conservative town, she was in tears. She recounted that my brother had gone to a party on the beach that night with his hoodie on. They had fought about him taking it off. He wanted it on for style. She wanted it off for safety. "You are the only Black boy at this party. The last thing you need is for someone to think you are up to no good." News of Trayvon broke the next morning. It rattled the both of them to the point of tears at the breakfast table. My fourteen-year-old brother apologized to her. She was just trying to save his life.

My brother felt like my baby. Big age gaps can do that. The thought of him being scared or unfairly treated would move me into big sister mode fast. The fact that he was now unsafe *to be*—to choose what clothes he wanted to wear, where he might be walking at night—felt violating. Infuriating. And, frankly, hopeless. But I wasn't the only person feeling like that. The entire student group who had led Martin Lee Anderson pro-tests, now spread out around the nation holding various jobs, were on call by night's end. More miraculous in retrospect than it ever felt then, everyone left what they were doing—their jobs, their respective cities—and came home. Back to the heat. Back to the palm trees. Back to the flared tempers and distaste for our "rebel" rousing. Florida denied justice for Martin. They wouldn't do that to Trayvon. We couldn't let them. Our reasons were all the same: this could be our kids one day. For me, it was for my baby.

Sybrina Fulton and Tracy Martin, Trayvon's father, were always at anything organized to demand justice for Trayvon in the early days. Sybrina's hair was always in micro-braids, the type we Black women wear when we are going on vacation or traveling for an extended period and don't have time to worry about our hair. She *didn't* have time to worry about her hair and she was traveling a lot. But nothing joyous was attached to her trips. In an almost uniform slacks and dress shirt every time we saw her, she would barely speak. We thought her quiet. Years later we would recognize she was in a daze, reeling and grieving and wishing she could retreat to her bedroom and never turn the lights on again. Instead she had to be where we were. To ensure her son's killer didn't walk free.

Tracy Martin always spoke. He would remember even the smallest details. If you had a cold the last time he saw you, he'd remember to ask how you were feeling today. He, like Robert Anderson, was tall. It was the first thing you noticed. Unlike Robert, he was broad-shouldered. Fitted baseball caps and matching shirts and sneakers, he was exactly what Miami looked like. If you weren't from Florida, you might mistake it as "urban"; a sheltered white person may even be slightly fearful. If you were from the state, however, he was a normal if not well put together young father. And you'd bet his sons were "good boys." Like Robert, his now deceased son was also tall. Trayvon had not yet put on grown man weight, but his build suggested he would. He was precisely what you would have expected the son of Sybrina and Tracy to be. Trayvon was their baby.

They supported all the protests. They spoke eloquently and passionately. I watched them grow tired but never waver. I would watch Sybrina, like Gina before her, never flinch. Speak assuredly. In the very early days, she cried almost every time she opened her mouth. A few months in and she almost never allowed her voice to crack. Like Gina, she would always look someone in the eye. They both would stand almost cat-like; if someone were to say the wrong thing, they were ready. Gina's presence had been intimidating. She had little patience left for the folks in Florida and would not suffer fools. Sybrina was graceful. You would watch people whose minds were made up that *Trayvon was a thug who got what he deserved* meet her and walk away changed. Her very presence moved hearts. She wouldn't cry or yell or speak ill of anyone. To this day she won't utter the name of the man who killed her son. Even her sworn opposition would promise her their help. Those that didn't want to give in to the fact that Trayvon was murdered would simply say, "I hope she gets some kind of justice," and leave to deal with their own cognitive dissonance.

Sybrina came to know each of us activists well. If someone were missing from an event, she'd ask for them by name. My proximity to her attorneys made us closer. Eventually, we were all a family. By the time the trial came around I was no longer on the ground in Florida. I had gone back to Los Angeles to plan my wedding. She had insisted on meeting my fiancé. And grilled him.

When the "not guilty" verdict came down, our hearts, like the collective hearts of most of the country, were shattered. We feared for our babies—my baby brother—and for the Black men in our lives. My best friend, also one of the former activists for Martin Lee Anderson, was the legal consultant for the Orlando local news. She knew, after watching the case closely, that there was likely no chance the jury would return a guilty verdict. And she said that on air. Then went into her car and called me to cry. I was in London, returning in just a few hours. We cried together. I cried through my taxi ride to the airport and through security. As I sat, waiting to board, several Black people came to hug me. They cried too. One very sweet Brit came and handed me a coffee: "Move to London, sweets. We'd never let that happen here."

It was a double loss for us who knew Sybrina and Tracy. Not only was this a monumental case, it was the single most important thing to people we love dearly. None of us knew how to approach them. I especially didn't know how to approach her. The case had drudged on for so long that by the time it was all over, a national movement had begun. Some protestors had started a brand-new community organization and relocated. Some had gone on to run national organizations. Some had just moved on. There was no central meeting place for everyone who had been involved in the fight to go and discuss how to support each other or Sybrina and Tracy now. We all just called and texted each other, and wondered when we would physically see either of them next. If we should wait until we saw them to say anything. Should we call? Should we text? Was it better to say nothing at all? For the first time since his death, she was given a moment to herself because no one knew what to do. In that time, she not only was able to grieve her son, but also the injustice. Like Gina, she had to live, every day, knowing her baby would never get the justice he deserved.

Because he was still her baby. He was gonna be her baby 'til she died.

* * *

As my son Ryder lay in my arms and used my neck as a human nail file, I wondered what Sybrina remembered about Trayvon as a baby. Do you forget these wolverine moments? Did he have some tic? Could she even think about it now? How awful to have to put beautiful memories away. She hadn't seen me throughout my pregnancy, though she texted often and commented on all my Facebook pictures. It wouldn't be until I was six months pregnant and she came to Los Angeles that we would meet up at a gala for the National Bar Association.

I almost skipped the event. My feet were swollen, and I was tired. I had nothing to wear and felt unfit for a black-tie evening. It had been three years since we marched in Sanford and met Sybrina. I was married now. Not that that made you more of an adult but it kind of did. And adult me felt like I had too much responsibility and far too little sleep to attend. Becoming a parent certainly illuminated adulthood. The banquet was honoring Ben Crump and Daryl Parks. I had all the reason in the world to go, but I felt like they would understand if I skipped it. Sybrina pestered. Incessant texts and calls. She wasn't asking me to be at the gala. She was telling me to be there.

"You're not *that* big in person. You look bigger in your pictures."

"That's not a compliment, Sybrina."

She greeted me at the door of the ballroom that night, some twenty minutes after I texted her from the bathroom that I was there, but keeping my legs elevated in a stall to take my ankle swelling down.

Every time Sybrina texted during my pregnancy she would talk about her kids. The stories and anecdotes were from a seasoned mother of two rambunctious boys whom she had seen successfully through to adulthood. Until her baby's life was cut short.

We never spoke about it like that. We talked about it like mothers. Like all children were present, both hers that had died and mine who was not yet born. I never said much about it, although it always touched me. She was a mother of two. She *is* a mother of two. She had done a damn good job. Jahvaris, her oldest, was smart and ambitious, funny, and a great friend. It would be hard to believe that Trayvon would have been much different from stories we had been told and from knowing her and Tracy. I would talk about my uncertainty in a way that makes sense for a mother who has not yet met her child. In some ways having one of her children pass away made Sybrina understand the unknown more. When she saw me, she ran and grabbed me. The type of hug you give someone you've been waiting to hug. The black ties and evening gowns around whispered about who Sybrina was. I could never tell if she was oblivious to people staring at her in a room or if she just didn't care. There was no personal space. Sybrina and the women from Parks and Crump Law Firm were all hands-on-belly. Laughing and hugging. In some ways I was their baby. And now their baby was having a baby.

Sybrina and I sat behind each other that night so she could sneak me extra food. When everyone got up to mingle, I went and sat by her. We talked about my morning sickness. My plans for childcare. How I was feeling in general.

"When I was pregnant with Tray everyone called me fat mama. I was big. You are not that big. But that doesn't mean that baby won't be big."

"What was delivery like for you?"

"Girl, you forget. Kind of. With Tray it was . . . "

She re-lived the birth of Trayvon. What he was like as a baby in comparison to Jahvaris. She spoke with knowing. With confidence. Helping me. Guiding me. Teaching me how to be a good mommy as she had been.

Although she was dropping knowledge, the kind of information new moms soak up when someone sits and talks to them about their impending journey, at some point I stopped listening. In the years of fighting for justice, protesting, and sharing images of hoodies up and #RIP it only hit me that night that the same kicks and movement I felt in my stomach she had felt, too. All the hopes and dreams and thoughts of the future I held for my son she had held for hers. Someone stole all of that. She was so close to seeing him become the man she had raised. She was looking forward to watching him thrive and her chance was lost. In a moment. Sybrina had seen Trayvon through teething and first steps; she was telling me about it. He had been grounded for bad grades and talking back. ("Let them know you aren't playing young.") He had been celebrated for touchdowns and cleaning the dishes. She was so proud of him.

We were defending his name from those who were trying to justify their dislike for a child they didn't know. She was defending the baby she carried, whom she knew so intimately. An intimacy I was just learning. I was paralyzed. This was different than fighting for your baby brother. That love is real and palpable and special. A type of love siblings know and close friends can mimic. But losing—and fighting for—your child is different. It's fighting for a part of yourself not to die. Then, not to be forgotten or treated as inhuman.

When my son would pinch my neck, I'd think of the night at the gala. Every time. I had to learn to not imagine going through what she had. The thought would make me nauseous. I would sit and hum "Something Inside So Strong" to my baby. A song taught to everyone who had ever set foot near the Children's Defense Fund or gone to their Freedom Schools:

> *The more you refuse to hear my voice*
> *The louder I will sing*
> *You hide behind walls of Jericho*
> *Your lies will come tumbling*
> *Deny my place in time*
> *You squander wealth that's mine*
> *My light will shine so brightly*
> *It will blind you*

Sybrina and Tracy had sung Trayvon's praises to the mountaintops. They repeated the story of him saving his father's life in a house fire. His mentorship. His grades. His bright countenance. They explained to the world that, despite his height, he was a kid. And he was their baby. Many people couldn't comprehend that. They saw a grown man who had smoked weed and died at the hands of a vigilant community watchmen. They couldn't see him as a kid or their baby. Their distance gave them a caricature on TV; their inability to touch them made Sybrina, Tracy, and Trayvon two-dimensional. Personalities that fit pre-conceived notions and long-held biases that a twenty-second snippet on the nightly news could never undo. The general white public couldn't always receive Sybrina's information. At that point, I realized no one *really* could. The only people who could come close to fathoming what she had lost were parents. People who had children since they were unable to open their eyes for longer than a few moments and depended on you entirely for survival. People who had squealed at first words and cried at school plays. Who had cried in their bathrooms after doing what they thought was right to raise a healthy human and being stricken by the fact that they might get it wrong. People who kissed boo-boos and snotty faces and risked every virus known to man to comfort their kids. Whose hearts dropped when they heard the words, "Are you the mother of..." For most of us those last words meant a broken bone or a behavior problem. For Sybrina and Tracy, those words are different.

I wrestled those thoughts every night for the first year of my son's life. One night, while those chubby hands attacked my neck, my thoughts attacked me. My heart overflowed with love and guilt; I oscillated between feeling resolute in protecting him and sickened by the reality that I couldn't protect him from much. The world decided who he was long before they ever met him. When he was finally asleep, my neck welted, I texted Sybrina and told her that now that I was a mother, I respected her so much more. I couldn't appreciate her correctly when I was a single woman without children. I couldn't feel the weight of her loss because I had never felt the weight of that love. I thanked her for being the way she was. I apologized that the system had denied her justice. It was not my apology to give. But, like so many others, I offered up what I could. Someone had to.

She only responded that she loved me. And to kiss my son. I did. I kissed him for her, for Gina, and for me.

«THREE»

BLOODLINE
OF A NAME

Only my mother's name is on my birth certificate. Her signature, the not-so-neat and girlish scribble of someone barely a woman, is written "Jennifer Ann-Marie Baden." The line for father is left blank. My name is hers. Vanessa Jennifer Baden. I couldn't take a surname of someone unknown. Her name is not her own. My mother was born on the tiny island of Seychelles, tucked away some thousands of miles off the coast of Madagascar. An East African, Francophone nation that was so uniquely placed—so far removed from the mainland—that it's often left off traditional maps. A place coveted for ritzy vacations and beautiful photos yet still forgotten in name and place by the people to whom she belongs. A place not much unlike myself.

In Seychelles, my mother was a Didon. There, my mother was born out of wedlock to my grandmother, Jeannine, who was also barely a woman. She carried my grandma's last name for the same reasons I did. In a place like Seychelles, colorism was rampant but classism loomed as large and your surname was evidence of your place on the socio-economic food chain. Even if a person should have darker skin or crepe hair, there was yet some grace for you in polite society should your surname reflect upper class lineage. My grandma, to this day, reminds us that though our last name was Didon that we are, by lineage, Sauzier.

Being a Sauzier is important. They are doctors and business people. They are also fairer skinned, but that was somewhat of an afterthought. My grandma's grandpa was a Sauzier. He was a Frenchman that took residence on the island. He had a wife. And children. And like many of the Europeans who inhabited the island, first the French then British, he had children by one of his Black domestic workers. Their daughter, my great grandmother Arice, would not live with her own Black mother but with her father. Her mother's hope, of course, that her last name and fairer skin would pivot her from poverty and domestic work to something better. Something more substantive than packed dirt floors and aluminum roofs that prick, prick, pricked under rain. But her father would also not give her his last name. He would have her take her mother's—his wife not fond of the child of an extra marital affair—and she would be relegated to the barn, only allowed to come inside to tend to her sisters—siblings whose names she would not only never share but who would never call her by her own. Instead of Arice, they called her "le petit negress."

The blood running through her veins was of no consequence to her family. Her blood didn't make her family. It was about what they called her. Like Arice, my grandmother and mother would carry the surname Didon until my grandfather—who we all affectionately called Papa—arrived.

Like me, my mother's birth certificate had an empty line and a child's signature. Unlike me, Richard E. Baden's block letters, written by a typewriter in some embassy or remote government office, would naturalize her and make her both an American and a Baden, leaving no empty lines. The original document would always be traceable. Enough family tree searching and probing through the internet and you could find traces of who she was before his surname was added. But none of it would matter. Everything important now, from school enrollment to the birth of her children, would identify her as Jennifer A. Baden. She was forever changed. I would always be who I was. One signature short. Papa would always be who he was: the signature filler. I had his name too. And his house. His breakfast. His taxiing to school and groups and friends' houses. I knew it was better to have both signatures, that my surname shouldn't be his. But that last name saved me from knowing what that could truly look like.

* * *

BEFORE WE LEARN HOW TO SAY I'm sorry or I'm happy, when cries are all we know to demand life's basic necessities, we learn our names. We learn when to look back or look around, before our eyesight is sharp enough to discern images or our hearing clear enough, not garbled—like the underwater garble of amniotic fluid—when someone says our name. Our names are our birthright whether or not we have the right to much else. When we first learn to write, before we can phonetically sound out words or string together simple sentences, we learn to write our name. Wobbly letters that slope outside of the blue and dashed perimeters of our elementary paper until we learn to keep it within the lines. We don't know what each individual letter represents or the sounds they make, but we understand that the exact location of each letter, grouped just so, represents "me." First. Middle. Last. Suffix if there were one. Words that represent a living, breathing human. More than an object like a ball or a loaf of bread, names are vaster than an idea. Books can be written about the theory of relativity and that theory never changes—maybe it will be later expounded upon, but the idea and explanation thereof are finite. A name represents something ever-evolving. A human who even upon their birth, should they have someone born of the same womb at the exact same moment— would be wildly different—with a different destined death, love, and life trajectory. The way we would determine whose life was who would be by name. A full name is both a story constantly being written and an ever-changing history. The name "Ashley" may be an identifier of the person and the future they hold but the surname tells us a specific history. What makes *this* Ashley different than that one. Where she was born, who she was born from—those details determine so many more possibilities of her life.

Somehow, it doesn't seem like the unique mix of first, middle (should there be one), and surname should hold so much weight. It seems as though naming a boy "John Smith" should have less impact on his person than whether or not he was born in Jamaica or Detroit, to a single mother or nuclear family, into wealth or abject poverty. All those things certainly matter. As does the person's race, cultural background, and all other signifiers. But the name is too often overlooked. Names allow us to be interjected into something that is already established. They are our personal SKU—scanned by society so they can tell us on what shelf we belong. Our birth certificates serve as our tag: vitals, where we were made, the company that made us. When a line is empty, we seem generic. Our names tell the world if we are a luxury or knock off. What clan or family or institution we belong to is etched in eternal record at the exact same time we arrived on earth, but whether the world knows that record depends on our name. Those of us lucky enough will be born into a group that will allow for us to see our names on family cards and plane tickets to family reunions or college acceptance letters. Those not so lucky will never know from whom their surname came. Or will have it replaced with "Doe." Worse, they might have it replaced all together—exchanged for a number—and count the sleeps until the day they can see it again. If ever.

* * *

As a child I would copy the neat script of my grandfather's name. Every line and curve of "Richard E. Baden" was memorized by the time I was four years old. That was the only thing Papa would write in cursive. Everything else was small, rounded, and fully capitalized. He told me once that he never really learned to write in cursive. It was taught, and he remembered it vaguely but didn't really know it. He worked on his family's chicken farm after the Depression and learning squiggly letters seemed less important than learning to neatly print the contents of the day on sheets for inventory—in block so they couldn't be misunderstood. I once read that people who write in all capital letters suppress their emotions. Both are probably true. Papa always told me that he considered cursive fancy and regal and meant for really important documents, so long as it is legible. So I learned his name in cursive before I could write in print. I rushed to learn cursive, trying to attach my letters before we were taught so I could write my name in cursive. My written hand is in cursive until this day. It is not legible.

When I would think of my grandpa's handwriting, I always thought of those block letters. But when I thought of his name I thought of cursive. There was no other way to see it written. Until his hospital room. Papa's name was in block, capital letters on his hospital room. But he didn't write it. A nurse had. I never saw it in person because I never went back to Florida while he was hospitalized. Cancer came quickly. One day he was fine. The next he wasn't. Stage 4 cancer was a sudden shock to my family but generally didn't seem like something out of the blue for an almost 87-year-old man. Somehow, generalities never apply when you are in the moment. Especially when it comes to death. When death arrives for someone you love, it always feels new, and startling, and unfair. Even if you've seen it coming a mile away. Both of my grandparents assured me that no matter the prognosis, he would not stay hospitalized. Live or die it would be at home. So they checked him out when it was clear nothing more could be done. He was given six months to live. The doctors signed the prescriptions with their names. The nurses signed their reports with their names. And my grandfather signed his discharge papers with his. I only know because I saw them when I was going through his paperwork, preparing for the funeral.

When someone dies, those same words of their name, letters arranged the exact same way, suddenly transform. First, middle, and last. They now represent what was. The evolution has stopped. There are no more futures attached to the name, with the exception of the changes that the living may have to endure as a result of the loss. The name will no longer appear on the check-out sheet when the school nurse calls and says you're sick. Now they fill new lines. In loving memory of. On tombstones. Death certificates. Those finite words now represent the finite. They will never be written again for what is. Only who we will remember. Those memories created the meaning and fullness of the surnames—the family lineage to whom they will be passed down. And that passing does not always happen by blood.

* * *

We called my husband's grandpa Paw Paw, and to Paw Paw I was a Kelly, long before I was legally a Kelly. He didn't care that I or any of us married-into Kellys weren't born into the family or that he hadn't known us since birth. What he cared about was the carrying of the family name. Even the granddaughters whose names had been exchanged for that of their husbands were still Kellys; their families were new off-shoots of a rich legacy. His legacy.

Paw Paw's voice was deep. Like my father-in-law and both my husband and son. My son's baby voice was always distinctly deep. The day he was born the nurses noted how low his cry was compared to the other babies. We knew who was crying in the nursery before we saw who it was. That was passed down. As was his size. He was (and is) destined to be as big as his great-grandfather. Paw Paw was tall and broad chested and could only be described as "big," in stature and in presence. He was the middle of seventeen children and knew that College Station, Arkansas was not big enough for him. When he moved to Kansas City, Missouri (a distinction must be made between Kansas City, Missouri and Kansas City, Kansas because natives will tell you they are two totally different places) he would pave most of the sidewalks. He would desegregate the unions. He would be the only Black person in his community to have an in-ground swimming pool. Everyone knew the name James E. Kelly. My husband and I made our son his namesake. Even if our boy had his size and voice and even his blood, we understood the value of sharing his name.

When I was pregnant with my son, my husband and I knew we wanted to name him after Paw Paw to carry on the legacy of his name. My husband's eldest uncle was Paw Paw's junior. He had a son, also named James E. Kelly, whom we call Trey. Still, we wanted our child to share it. To bear the name of someone we thought great. To have eternally ingrained in record our adoration for Paw Paw. So he could see it and it could live beyond him. We weren't sure if we would choose Paw Paw's first name, James, or his middle name, Ellis. We decided on James. Ellis would be our second who would be named after both of our grandpas, Papa and Paw Paw. Richard Edward and James Ellis. Both were alive when we were deciding on names. Now the name we write every day on lunch boxes and preschool applications is the only name that lives. Its sake does not.

The memory of their names that sticks out the most to me, the memory eternally etched into my mind, is looking at the letters on the slide shows of both of their funerals. The first, RICHARD E BADEN. The words arranged in the order I had written them since I first learned to write. Since he had taught me to write. And I couldn't comprehend how the words "In loving memory" stood before them. I couldn't make sense of how this name had changed. How suddenly words I'd always written now meant something so different.

The funeral arrangements fell on my eldest uncle and me. When you are in charge of helping everyone else grieve, your grief leaks out in spurts and mostly at inopportune times. I had arranged the program, the order of events for the day. We found the caterer for the repass and folded two hundred green ribbons per my grandma's request. I had arranged the table with his ashes and his favorite straw hat. In the back of the church I was loading the slide shows and music. I had been going nonstop since the moment I landed in Florida, staying up until 2 a.m. the night before finishing everything for the next day. My best friend drove from over an hour away to bring me something to wear for the service. On her own lunch break, she went to the mall, bought three dresses in my size, and drove them to my grandparents' home so I would have something to put on. She had arrived around 10 p.m. the night before, after she got off and ate dinner. She stayed with me while I finished, so she could feed my son bottles of breast milk. That next day, I was equally as busy, until I tested the slide show. Watching the name projected on the screen brought me to my knees. I could vividly remember him teaching me how to write my own name. Him teaching me a million other things. I collapsed in the church. The facilities manager held me up until I could support myself. I must have been there about twenty minutes before someone quietly whispered that my family would be there soon, and we were not done. To continue, I asked them to not turn on the screens until I had dressed and met my family in the atrium. For the rest of the day I avoided looking at his name.

When my husband's Paw Paw died, I saw the name James E. Kelly written in the same memory as Papa's had been two years earlier. That gnaw I had been able to successfully push down until the final moments before the funeral of my own grandpa began to subtly nibble on every nerve ending. I didn't dare give in to them. I wasn't sure what compounding grief might feel like. I hadn't shared a bloodline with either of them. One had raised me while the other met me when I was twenty-six. But both had chosen to be my family. They had chosen me. Both had spoken life into me. Both had given me grace, encouragement, and love. Both had transitioned from a finite body to something else. Someplace else. But both names remained. Attached to me until the end of my own time. Attached to my children. And to their children. Their stories of going AWOL from the army to chase a good time in Texas or traveling around the country singing gospel with their brothers would outlive them.

I sat on the front row of this funeral too. This one different. A casket in place of an urn. I watched as my husband diverted his eyes, the same way I had. He stared forward, watching the feet of everyone who passed after having paid their respects. I knew what he was doing, and I knew why. I watched my father-in-law, who would officiate the homegoing celebration, tap his feet in time to the music playing. He was a consummate professional, too. He welcomed everyone who came to say goodbye. He also diverted his eyes. I wondered if everyone knew something I hadn't. I had stared at the name projected. They somehow knew better. I scanned the building, looking for my own son. He was one of the few children there and hard to miss in a toddler-size black suit and bouncing curls. He sat with my mother-in-law and her husband near the back of the church. She had him wave at me. I watched as in an almost-perfect alignment, he sat angled between his grandpa and his father. Both men at the same angle in a different direction. Almost center, the earliest of the generations, saying goodbye. I wondered if this was all different for them than it had been for me. To watch generations there together, sharing lineage and DNA. I didn't know any other grandpa. I didn't know any other father. Losing Papa was equal to losing a parent for me. But I couldn't help but wonder if that blank line on my birth certificate had made my pain less. Was the bond somehow less without blood?

* * *

I MET MY PATERNAL GRANDMOTHER EXACTLY one year before I met Paw Paw. She didn't know who I was when we met. My mother was pregnant at seventeen. She never mentioned my father until I was twenty-five years old. Once, in kindergarten, all the children were talking about their fathers. Some were home with them. Some in the military traveling. Others divorced. When it was my turn, I shrugged. I had barely considered it. I lived with my grandparents. I saw on TV and from classmates that most people lived with a mom and dad in the household, but considering I was very happy and had so much fun, I surmised that while that must be the MOST normal, it probably wasn't the only way to grow up and hadn't thought much beyond that. So the question of who my father was baffled on two fronts: his actual identity and why I had never asked the question myself.

"Vanessa, where is your dad?"

"I don't have one."

The day care teacher cackled with her Newport-worn voice. Her name was Miss Donna and her daughter was in my grade. "Everyone has a dad. You probably just don't know who yours is."

The answer to the question I had never asked was simple: there was another half of me, but I didn't know his name. I didn't carry his name. I was barely named myself. My mother wasn't sure she was going to keep me with the volatility that her pregnancy created. Before I was born, she would move from my grandma's house. They couldn't get along. Their versions differ but the crux was the same: no one was ready for there to be a me. So I had no name. No proper clothes. No place to sleep. When I came home from the hospital, there was a flurry to prepare for the baby that shouldn't be. Our neighbor, Mrs. Madigan, brought her family bassinet over for me to sleep in. With my birth it became the neighborhood bassinet. It was white with delicate lace around the perimeter. Fancy for a baby with little else awaiting their arrival. Much more plush than the simple plastic bassinet that read "Baby Baden" in the hospital. I wouldn't get the name Vanessa until it was almost time to be discharged. My mother heard her cousin say he would name his child Vanessa if he ever had one. She stole the name. But, as repayment, she made him my godfather. My mom gave me her own first name as my middle. A fatherless child carries her mother's surname. I carried my mother's first and last. I came home to her family. I was loved and raised by her family. For a child who knew nothing of reproduction and human anatomy, they could have told me that I was dug up behind the mango tree and I would have believed it, because the mango tree was a Baden staple and so was I. Both of us belonged there. My nose was a little different than everyone else's. My butt a little higher. I had freckles. Fuller lips. But beyond that I was a spitting image of my mother; our baby pictures made it difficult to determine who was who. Without a different name—the only indicator a five-year-old might have that they are different—there was no way to tell.

Beverly Cohens was my father's mother's name. By marriage. She had been married once before to a man named Richard. They had one child. She divorced her first husband due to "extreme cruelty" and married my paternal grandfather, Franklin, a Black man in Mountain Home, Idaho in 1965. Beverly was white. I don't know any of these stories from their own mouths or family talks after Christmas dinner or late-night cups of coffee. I learned it all on the internet. I was never able to ask about how terribly unusual the proximity of her divorce date to her wedding date was and the subsequent birth of my eldest uncle. However these things happen, she became a Cohens in a time when she would essentially become a social outcast for being married to a Black man. And she accepted it. The two times I met her, she seemed more than happy to have this family and that name. Proud of the struggles they had overcome together. The first time I met her she had no clue who I was. My mother and my father had reconnected, as so many do, on Facebook. Within minutes of seeing her profile, he frankly asked her if I was his. He remembered her pregnancy in high school and asking her then. She flatly told him no. He alleges that he never believed her. Still didn't. He then attached a photo of his eldest (known) daughter. The resemblance was uncanny.

My mother vetted him for weeks. She hadn't seen him since they were in high school. She wasn't sure that I needed the stress of such a revelation, having only recently arrived in Los Angeles. I certainly didn't need his help, financially or otherwise. Her own family had been all that I needed. But she knew that I wanted to know. By this point the conversation, though avoided, loomed every few years. I was sitting on the hood of my 2006 Honda Civic when she told me. I left something on inside the car running errands and came back to a drained battery. It was hot in LA that day. The type of desert swelter that only happens for about a week or two a year and reminds residents that before there was a Walk of Fame, there was a direct route to the Mojave Desert. I didn't want to wait inside the mall where I had been for fear of missing roadside assistance, but I couldn't sit in my vehicle and be cooked. So I was on the hood. When she called and told me what she had learned and more—that he only lived an hour away in the Inland Empire—I climbed off the hood and sat in my car. She gave me his number. Told me I could call if I wanted. When we hung up, I was drenched in sweat and tears.

The ridiculous predicament that I was cast into from that point on was my lack of the Cohens last name. I might have had their blood (and they were even skeptical about that), but I was not a Cohens. They had known nothing about me as a child and I didn't share a surname, so I was not, and still am not, part of who they are. I drove to the Inland Empire a month or so later. My father and I had begun talking regularly and we decided a proper DNA test would be necessary. When I came for us to do it, he told me he would take me out to dinner. It was his youngest daughter's (my sister's) thirteenth birthday, and his family was all together to celebrate her at a local Mexican restaurant. I came with them. My father and I (and his girlfriend who was also there) had full knowledge of my relation to everyone at the table. No one else did.

Beverly was very nice when she met me. Kind even. She remembered my mom from the "tiny little town" in Florida her family had been stationed in for a few months while her boys were in high school. She remembered that they had dated. Beverly believed her son was showing an old friend's daughter around Southern California. My father later told me that she had warned him not to sleep with me.

"She's very pretty but way too young for you Shawn."

They shared stories freely at the dinner. There was no pretense or holding back information. I was a friend. There was no need to be up in arms. Beverly told stories of sending care packages to Franklin during the war, him asking for canned collards and her having no clue what those were and sending canned spinach. Or the first time he asked her to make macaroni and cheese and she lopped a block of cheddar in warm noodles, stirring it feverishly in hopes that it would melt. When Franklin finally saw her work, he asked her where she had learned this recipe. In her own frustration and embarrassment, she straightened up, brushed her hair back and said, "It's the Irish way."

I watched every face at that table and searched for myself in it. I stared intently at my father. His father. His daughter. Beverly. I wondered if I looked like them. Would I look like them. My mind was in such a flurry that I kept forgetting what I looked like and would have to sneak a look at a picture of myself on my phone and then attempt to compare features. I felt like I could hear my heartbeat in my ears the entire night and tried to commit each story I heard—cadences of voices, lines on faces—to memory. I kept meaning to ask how "Cohens" was their last name. If someone might be Jewish. It seemed unlikely. It was passed down from my grandpas' side and he was Black from New Jersey. Black folks can't really tell how we got our last names.

Eventually, they would find out my alleged kinship and I would never speak to any of them again. Once it was revealed that there was a chance that I was family they balked at the idea of a newcomer and threatened to have nothing to do with my father if he had anything to do with me. So he didn't. He owed them quite a bit. He had a rough go as a younger man, and from what I could tell hadn't recovered entirely. The only thing that effectively kept him on his feet when was them. As family does.

Several different women had claimed he fathered their children over the years. They had not granted a test to any of them. They were not Cohens. The only children of his they accepted were the ones by women he married. The one I looked like and the one who's birthday dinner I had attended, though they had different mothers. The eldest hated how they enabled her father's bad behavior and would become distant from her paternal family, clinging more to her mother's side. The youngest would fall into the fold and the sisters eventually also became distant. I didn't know any of that then. I just knew that communication stopped. Not all at once, but it was sharp. I didn't fully notice. After the DNA test I waited for weeks for the results. I Googled and called and asked anyone I could what was the longest wait one might have to endure for the results of paternity. When we flew past that mark, I asked my father what the results were. I was nervous I wasn't his child, and he was too sad to tell me.

"I messed up the test. We will have to do it again someday."

Someday never came. He stopped calling. So did I. His girlfriend asked my mother to stop reaching out. And we discussed amongst ourselves that it was probably for the better. It wasn't until I had my own son, and the pesky questions of "family medical history" had entire rows blank—the blank line that had also plagued me—that I decided to reach out again. The radio silence was deafening. I remembered his eldest daughter's name and found her on social media after attempts of reaching out to every other member of my family went checked (the messages would show that they had been read) and never responded to. I wrote her a long letter in her private messages. I told her who I was. How I met everyone except her. How I didn't need anything but information. She first responded with:

"Wait. Who are you?"

I explained again. A day or two went by.

"I asked everyone about your story. Everything you are saying is true. I know you met my grandparents and my sister and my dad. And I know they don't want anything to do with you. I think that's messed up."

We talked for months before we decided to do the DNA test. She showed me pictures of her grandparents growing up. Our siblings. She shared stories and lineage. I came to find Beverly had passed away the year I was married, two years after meeting her. I had no idea. I had no contact. I don't know how she died, but I know it hurt my sister who still seemed like she was grieving. I understood that.

Both of us almost chickened out of taking the DNA test several times. The confirmation of my lineage confirmed and undid so much for us both. It confirmed my story, making people she loved dearly and held in high regard culpable of treating a blood relative very badly. It confirmed for me that I could have known this family all along, perhaps sharing their name and never having to feel the rejection they hurled. It undid for her the idea that she knew her family inside and out. There was so much more, so many more layers that she not only didn't know but would be complicit in secret-keeping if she didn't make it her business to find out. It undid the idea for me that I was a one-sided person. I was not asexually made and there was a need for me to know more of a family that had no interest in my knowing them.

The Cohens refused to speak to her because she entertained "the lies of a stranger." But I wasn't a stranger. She went on to post our 99.999% DNA match on social media. To vindicate me from their calls of "wanting something" and to separate herself from them. I was not a "Cohens" but I was still family to her. I was her sister. That bloodline mattered. I had their name etched into my veins even if it wasn't legal. I was and remain so thankful for my sister, thankful that she stood up to everyone and stood up for me because she could feel in her bones—a genetic makeup we shared—that we were kin. I was so relieved that she was right. The embarrassment and ridicule she would have faced had her intuition been wrong might have been over-whelming. There would have been so little I could have done at that point. I would have been relegated to family friend and resident shit-starter and she would have been held accountable for trying to do what was right. For being the family of someone who was searching for one. It brought me back to my grandfa-thers. To Papa. To Paw Paw. My bloodline had never mattered to them. They gave me their name with little knowledge beyond knowing someone they loved loved me and they loved me too. To them, I was family even when I wasn't. To my own blood I could never be family even when I was.

* * *

AT PAPA'S FUNERAL, THE SLIDESHOW PLAYED to the 300 people there. It was standing room only. I had spoken with Papa the night before he died. We talked about my coming home in a week or two. I was a new mom and didn't have enough breast milk stored to leave the baby and couldn't travel with him because he already had his first cold. Papa assured me there was no rush.

My Grandma said: "Look at him. Does it look like you need to rush home?"

It didn't. He was on the love seat in our family room, bathrobe clad, eating and watching Family Feud. In Florida, most family rooms are actually what architecture calls Florida Rooms: two walls that connect to the rest of the home and one wall that is entirely windows. It was still daytime there. He couldn't use Facetime well and brought the camera nearly to his face to hear me. His cornea was all the camera could see. The light from the sun shining through the windows made his eyes look the stormiest color of grey. The type of grey that encompasses Florida every summer day at two in the afternoon for exactly forty-five minutes, downpours, and then the sun peeps out. I remember the color of his too close eyeball seeming breathtaking. As though I had never seen them that color before. I took a mental note to not forget the shade of grey his eyes were. We knew we were close to the end, our time finite, and I wanted to remember as much as I could. The conversation quickly moved on to what car we should buy now that we had a new little family. What was reliable. What would last us. I remember hating that conversation. I knew whatever car I bought would outlast him. But we had it. And pretended things were normal. Papa promised to circle some things in *Consumer Reports* and send it to me on Monday.

He died the next morning. On that couch. In that room. Looking out of the windows of the Florida Room. He was surrounded by my uncle, his wife, my mom, and my brother. Everyone tells me it was a gorgeous day outside. One of the prettiest they had seen in a long time. When he passed away, surrounded by his family—both blood and not—he looked outside and gazed at the gorgeous Florida weather. My uncle said it seemed like he was looking past that. The *Consumer Reports* he had for me was dog-eared on the dining room table. Today it sits dog-eared in my closet. I've since bought the car, but I don't know if it's what he circled. I never opened it.

I wasn't there, a fact that plagues me to this day. I can never decide if I should have been less stringent about breastfeeding and baby care and prioritized a little differently, or if it was better that I wasn't. That his death was not my last memory. That my infant didn't add chaos to that moment. What I do know is that before they took his body to the funeral home where they kept him until I could pay my respects, dozens of people came to see him. On the couch. In his robe. Exactly seven of them had his last name. Two shared his blood. But they were all family. They all called him Papa. He considered them all his children: his nieces, his nephews, his relatives. It was a Sunday. They all stopped their day, their moment, their week and rushed to my grandmas. They touched him. Held him. Prayed over him. Wept.

When Papa passed my surname had changed. I added it to my maiden name so as not erase the great legacy of Papa and who he was. I was now Vanessa J. Baden Kelly. No hyphen. Neither name was more important than the other. They both represented a legacy I was not born into but was gifted to me. When Paw Paw passed, it seemed like a fog was over us and the city of Kansas City. Like Papa, mourners came from every end of the country. Hundreds. Everyone had a story of how he took care of them. Took them in. Carried them. We were all a tentacle of that legacy. I wondered what Beverly's funeral was like. How her family grieved. The amount of people and mourners of your death doesn't necessarily speak to your quality of life or what kind of human being you might have been, but I would argue it does speak to your impact. I wondered if the Inland Empire had shown up for her as the cities my grandpas had lived in did for them. I wondered, if not that, had family traveled from all over the country and felt lost at the prospect of her passing, as had happened here? If not that, had her children come, with their children, and their children's children and sat in the chairs she loved, eaten the foods she ate, and spoke lovingly of the woman who had loved them so heartily? I knew for certain I was not there. And no one like me—whose father was our father but was told he couldn't be—was in attendance. At the very least she had missed that and that made me sad for her, until I remembered she never wanted us there anyway.

At least once a week I have to see the name of one of our loved ones who have departed this life. Whether it's writing my son's name on another new water bottle or paying a student loan Papa so graciously co-signed, I see them. They are not forgotten. I live in a city where Beverly is written everywhere. Hills. Center. Grove. I never think of her. I never associate that name with anything more than what I ever had. Maybe her children do. Or her grandchildren. Her real family. The people who she kissed goodnight and cried over. The people who cried over her death. Who see her name written and can't believe that it represents someone who was and now is not. Who diverted their eyes like I foolishly never did.

It is all inconsequential. Those are the things in life that no matter how important they are (or seemingly are) we cannot control. Family is who embraces you. Who walks with you through the trenches of life and who carries you when you are too wobbly to walk yourself. Sometimes those people have a shared name or a traditional familial extension. Sometimes they don't. That's not to say that blood shouldn't matter—it should. That is the family you don't get to choose. But blood can't be the only thing. It is not the only thing. It can come out of your veins but that doesn't mean it comes from your heart, and that is where family lives. That's because family is who we love enough to sacrifice for. Our comforts, our projected life, our time. Two people chose to sacrifice for me. One person didn't. All now gone. All mourned. But not all by me.

FOUR

UNRELIABLE NARRATOR

I sat in a sterile, white room where fluorescent lights highlighted the paneled ceiling. It felt more like an operating room than a classroom. When I decided to do this, to bet on myself and become a better writer, I had imagined the red-orange brick and open courtyards of my undergraduate degree. I thought there would be intellectual conversations abounding, book recommendations among milling creatives eager to share their "journey" and "voice" and every other buzz word that came with being a writer. Zora Neale Hurston would probably be there. And a young Baldwin. I would lap up their knowledge through spirited discourse with young Faulkners and Hemingways.

Instead I was in a corporate building converted into a university on the corner of Slauson and the 405 in Culver City. Brilliant writers were undoubtedly among us, but they were like me. They were too something to be in the brick and columned buildings that hosted the schools I dreamed of: too old or too Black or too poor to have devoted extra years and loans to a program that may never pay their bills. Writing was not terminal. We could not guarantee its promise of fame or fortune, let alone a paycheck. So to take this chance for us meant to do so economically if we wanted to do it at all. This was the place that "real" people came to learn to write. So the sterile wall and fluorescent lights should not have been my focus. My focus should have been the opportunity in front of me—the chance to earn a graduate degree with a one year old in my own city. The right to speak with authority in the writer's rooms where I worked and found myself so constantly behind the curve as they mentioned books and articles I had never heard of. The focus should have been my first workshopped piece, sitting in front of all of us. My first attempt at being a better writer—and human—than I was before I came. Fifteen months prior I had become a mother for the first time. Eight months prior to that my uterus had almost exploded from an undetected post-labor injury. I was working a dream job where I was the only person like me and felt both welcome and unqualified. I needed this space as much as I wanted it. But I was staring at the surgically bland walls, wondering what the hell I was doing here.

"Do you know what an unreliable narrator is?" he asked me.

"Yes." I replied.

"Do you understand what it means in the world of literature?"

I couldn't lie. I didn't want to lie. I didn't understand that. I knew what the words meant. I learned them in my public high school in Central Florida. I was incredibly intelligent. For a long time I didn't feel like I could even make that proclamation. If I said it around some folks they would think me a braggart—either because they knew themselves to be smarter because of the schools they attended or general conversations, or because they knew they weren't for the same reasons. I was in an odd in-between space where my race and pedigree didn't allow my person (so I felt) to speak for herself. My high school classmates went on to go to Harvard Law and NYU. I went to Florida State. Not for lack of brains or test scores, but because those schools are expensive and no one in my world had ever known someone to go off to school so far unless they were on athletic scholarship. I wouldn't even be able to go to a private school in Florida because my state sponsored academic scholarship didn't cover the entire tuition. I would go to the best (although University of Florida students may argue that point) public institution—the budget Ivy as we like to brag—and flourish there. I'd be brilliant there too. So smart and writing so much that I was often told to cut my work. "No one will read that much." But being the brightest at a school not considered a place for bright minds wouldn't earn me much by way of respect upon meeting new people or competing for jobs.

At Florida State, I fell in love with Toni Morrison. After reading *Beloved* in high school, I took a freshmen African American Literature course where I was asked to dissect *Sula* in an attempt to pass after missing too many classes (it was a 9 a.m. course and the professor ultimately passed me). Having to take apart those sentences, critique those characters, explore that world—one I actually knew intimately—I'd discover my voice. My voice was like Morrison. And Walker. And Lorde. And so many women I had never been shown or heard applauded. They spoke for me and the women and girls around me. I understood their syntax and cadences on a cellular level. They inspired me to tell my own stories. Those could be great. WE could be great and here lay proof. Chapters and chapters, volumes and volumes, Pulitzer Prize-sized proof. I quietly became a creative writing minor. Not a major because, obviously, people like me go to college to be able to work when they are done, and no one can ensure they will "work" in writing. But it was a small, rebellious move in following my heart and finding worth in my person, led by Ms. Morrison.

My first creative writing course, I arrived early. Other students had laptops; I had a bound composition book. But it was brand new. Purchased specifically for that course and for my future. The professor walked in after most of us, but not late. He was a short white man. A writer's belly draped in a red Hawaiian-print shirt. He wore a baseball cap and glasses and seemed to purposefully exude "bohème." I concluded this to be "writerly." He asked us each our favorite author. My answer came somewhere in the middle. Most people answered with names I had never heard of. He would engage—his favorite piece they wrote, a time he had met them at a retreat—until he got to me. I never doubted my answer. This was Toni Morrison after all. There was no hesitation in my answer. No one in the classroom seemed to think it unfounded, maybe they found it obvious for the only Black person in the class. I was certain my professor would say something about her, probably something I didn't know. I had readied myself to graciously accept all new information. My prepared answer was, "Wow, I didn't know that!" I wanted to ingest every morsel of new information with no ego. No fear of not knowing. I was betting on myself here. I had to be okay being the novice. He looked at me over his bushy brown and grey mustache. I waited for my first taste of literary knowledge.

"Fun fact: Morrison is the most overrated author there is. She's fine, but not that great. We say she is for a lot of political reasons"

A few other people chimed in both agreeing and disagreeing. I remember the ones who agreed were white boys who said they didn't understand. A white girl defended her staunchly. She was revolutionary. I can't remember those arguments because I knew I was transferring out of this class immediately. I had made a mistake. I wasn't a good writer because I loved Morrison. But I couldn't help that I loved her. Maybe modern literature was not what I loved. Maybe I loved swivel shelves at the end of the check-out aisle of the local grocery store or by the pharmacy at Walgreens. The literature that made you feel something but anyone with taste might know was a watery soup of words not worthy of study. If entering this world of creative writing meant I lost Toni Morrison, then maybe I didn't want it. I switched my minor to journalism. Hated it, but had enough credits between the two to get out with a minor in English with no discernible purpose. The beginning of that journey had taught me literary definitions like "unreliable narrator" but, as it ended so abruptly, I had never had to use it in critique. I wasn't sure I knew how to identify one in practice.

"No," I replied when asked if I knew how to use the term. "Not in the context of literature."

"I'll explain," he said. His voice seemed condescending to me. I pushed the thought down. I did not want to project on this white, graduate level professor and published author the same hurt that I felt in the undergraduate course years before. The truth was that the graduate professor in my new program *was* condescending, but not because he meant to be. I had seen him talking to people he actually liked and admired. He always spoke like that. He had resting bitch face of the larynx. There, of course, was the argument to be made that it was not just his voice but that he was condescending to everyone. I chose to believe the best of him. I had to. I couldn't be run out of another program. Especially not this time. It was his voice.

"Being a reliable narrator in our profession is imperative to telling good stories. We establish the narrator—first person, third person, whatever—as someone who is honest, who their audience can trust. The problem with your entire piece is that you are discussing perceived racism as truth. You cannot prove that. You cannot prove that any of these things happened to you because you are Black or a woman. You are showing yourself an unreliable narrator and, as an audience member, I now don't trust you. If you must write about this, you have to prove it. Otherwise, focus on the relationships. Make a scene…."

He continued, speaking for another five minutes or so. I tried to listen but found myself staring at the textured white of the walls. I listened to my thoughts instead. I didn't discredit what he was saying. Far the opposite, I took it all to heart. I heard my ego try to make the argument that he was wrong. My brain argued that he was right. He knew so much more than I did. Published. A carrier of all the info I wished to know. I coerced myself into listening again, scared that this brash man who I would never have another thing in common with would have some tidbit of style or craft that was actually precisely what I needed but I was missing it because he had bristled me. Was this writing? Did being here mean unlearning the things that moved me or inspired me? All those things were extensions of my experience. Did that mean I shouldn't be here? Had I made the same mistake again believing there was a space for a little Black girl—public school educated—in prose?

Submitted for First Writing Submission: 4.10.17—
Vanessa Baden—MFA Candidate

Keep a penny between your knees. Nothing is open past midnight but legs. Don't be fast.

The "Good Girl" subscribes to all of these things. These old wives' tales that are barely that because most spreading them have never been wives themselves. Not successful ones. Whatever that means. But they have all been taught to be good girls. To be the type of woman that a good Black man would want to marry. After all, you can't turn a hoe into a housewife. How would anyone know that she was a hoe if someone wasn't already desiring her?

* * *

A famous comedian paced across the stage to a mesmerized crowd. Beguiled by his truths dripping in sarcasm and monotone sanity, they waited for the next "someone had to say it" moment. He walked slowly across the stage. Without the slightest smile cracked, he uttered:

"Can we all stop pretending our grandfathers were great men and trying to model our relationships after our grandparents? Our grandpas were terrible men. They probably had another family. He probably hit your grandma. At best he was emotionally unavailable. Being a good husband is a new phenomenon that was born in the 1980s from *Family Ties*."

We laughed. Maybe to keep from crying but we laughed. We love our grandparents. There had been inklings and whispered stories of rumblings in their relationships and hard early years but that was of no consequence to us. They created our parents and were our parents' heroes. In many ways they were also our own. They are human and of course things weren't always perfect for them but consider the time. The culture. The space they were in.

The enslavement of human bodies creates voids in the human psyche that are not easily fixed in a generation or four. The mating of human bodies with no regard for their hearts, their personhood or their spirits creates voids in the human soul that have to be purposed to be fixed. After all, they were purposefully ripped apart. The conditioning that must take place to create fear in the hearts of a group enslaved but outnumbering their oppressor creates a new reality for the people enslaved. One that even upon being free will penetrate their minds, hearts, and families. Their normal will ultimately be a broken world. A place of broken hearts and broken families, steadfast in their resilience to overcome and hopeful in their ability to fight.

But still broken.

A woman in our class wrote a heartfelt piece about her own life. She was wiry, and blonde, and stylish in the way that said, "I'm cool but not so cool that I can't be serious." He liked her. To point that out seems unfair. Especially as a woman who is constantly judged by outward appearances. Plus, I never got the sense that he didn't *like* me. In fact, I think he did. The sense I got was that he already had preconceived notions of who he thought I was and stood for based on my writing, which was fair because I did the same based on his response. And to this woman based on her attire. In both my version and my graduate professor's version of this story, this part would be the same:

"He/She was nice enough. But his/her thoughts were those of a person with much to learn."

My professor's notes on her piece were, in my opinion, fair, and smart, and cracked it open in all the right places. He was so precise with his notes that I found myself envious of their exchange. He was the "tough" teacher of the MFA program. No one wanted him except those who felt like they had to "prove" that they were tough enough to take relentless critique and were not precious about their writing. No less than twenty times throughout the entire program would you hear some mention his name and not hear the sentence,

"I don't mind. I like that. I don't care if people are nice to me. Be mean. I want my work torn up. Tell me the truth."

Those close to me know that same sentiment to be the blocks on which my life was built. I not only want harsh truths but yearn for them—perpetually concerned that there is some deficiency somewhere that I do not have the resource to see. The faster it can be pointed out and corrected, the faster I can be better. Constantly improving for who, I have no clue. It wasn't for myself. The moment I reached a goal, the target moved. Further. Beyond the vast canyon I had just managed to scale or crawl through or climb over. I needed everyone around me to care enough to shoot me straight because the next hurdle of life was inevitable. It appeared the moment I over-came the one before it.

This was my first term, so I hadn't requested this professor. He was assigned me. When I learned of his reputation it felt like God was divinely aligning us. God knew what I needed. I was excited to have him, believing myself prepared and eager for someone to get to the bottom of my struggles in writing; to note me and tear me apart.

No one gives us that concession. We don't even give ourselves that concession. We don't often think of our lineage. Our true lineage, not what we pass down on our social media feeds to placate our families and appear upstanding to our too-nosey "friends." We don't consider that our father was the first male of a young mother and father. That perhaps he was the pride and joy, the thing that validated our grandmother because she "bore" her husband a son making her the perfect young wife. Grandaddy sure was proud of that. But his passion ran deep for the woman at the pool hall. Chattel slavery made passion and love separate. Should a man be forced to mate with another woman it would have no impact on his marriage. This was his job. His wife was what he sacrificed for. Good manners, a stable family, and being upstanding in society made Grammy not discuss the woman from the hall in polite society. But no amount of being the perfect wife and baring a beautiful son would slow down Grandaddy's passions. It was embedded. As it had been from his daddy before him. And before that. So her love was lavished on her boy. Even when her son did precisely what he saw his own father do to our mother, she protected his actions. Her son was something like her husband. Not perversion. Just deflected love.

Or maybe our mother was one of many. Close to her mother. A good girl. Upstanding. Did all she was told to do. She got her schooling. She excelled. She found a wonderful young man like her own father who was never unfaithful to his wife. She had children. Bought a house. Joined the Links. But when her heart yearned for more—for bigger sights, a new adventure, a deeper conversation, or connection—she was lightly chided. This. This is what we strive for. This is what life is. To put this in jeopardy is foolishness. This is what every girl wants. If she says she doesn't she's lying. Every girl wants to be married. Have a family. Settle down. Because most girls don't get this. Most girls get these two-timing good for nothings. You have accomplished so much. Marriage is an accomplishment. Children are an accomplishment. What else could you do that would eclipse this?

The way the professor noted the cool white woman was what I wanted. Her response is what I thought I was going to have. The tense but productive arguments they had on points of notes were masterful to watch. She knew her shit. Nothing on her page was fluff or undeliberate. If he questioned a choice she shot back with her reason. He'd consider and rebuttal. They came to places that pushed her writing in front of all of us. It was impressive and fruitful.

And hurtful. I couldn't have that discourse. I was an unreliable narrator.

I understood the cult-like fanfare over this professor from the people here who wanted to prove themselves tough. I was that person. I am that person still, although now, years later, I understand (in theory) that my worth is not tied up in how much abuse I can take. It never truly was a measurement of my mental fortitude, but rather a desire to show myself not weak. Truth is the most bitter of pills. Truth about something close to your heart, a truth that unclothes us and unmasks us and lays us bare at the feet of those who can trample us with the knowledge can feel like a moment of life or death. Our confidence—an ever-fragile attribute—is built on the notion that anything we know at any given time is true. A mix of our own due diligence and trust in the bearer of our information. It is why so many of us stay away from the truth or allow cognitive dissonance to win with no attempts to reconcile the inconsistencies. If we find out a core belief we have or some foundational knowledge we possess is not true or flat out wrong—what else don't we know? Have we been wrong? Have we hurt others or ourselves? It's frightening. Those of us who pride ourselves on being "seekers of truth" are just as scared. We abuse our confidence and intuition, bombard ourselves with "hard truths" in hopes of creating a solid foundation. One that no one can shake. A place where we can be safe from the tossing and churning of life's winds. We're trying to control the thing. Others are trying to ignore the thing. We're all afraid of the thing. It's all fear. Here, it was a fear that I didn't belong in a literary world. Since this was the only place I ever felt fully "suited"—a place where books were discussed freely through intellectual thought and ideas and disagreements were welcomed with no loss of love or respect, where we saw worlds in every imaginable way and all believed them because we trusted the author. Where could I be if not here? Inability to perform meant there was no place for me. But he told me I was untrustworthy. Unreliable. This woman knew how to be something I couldn't.

> Maybe it's something different all together. Maybe we were born of single parents. Maybe of split relationships. Maybe we are grandma's babies. Maybe we were no one's—raised ourselves and had to figure it out along the way. Still, if we follow the lineage we will end in the same place. We will meet at a jagged, splintered, disease infested boat, traveling

with the speed of the arms of 200 chained men in its under-carriage. Headed to anywhere in the diaspora where the story would inevitably unfold almost identical in thousands of countries around the world. We would be separated. Mated. And forced to take on a belief system that was not our own while secretly trying to maintain our own autonomy. Whenever release came in any respected country, we were judged by how well we could take on the culture of those who had entrapped us. No consideration was given that we had only been ever taught a twisted idea of what "proper" meant. We were fed a counterfeit version of their Christ. "Upstanding" to them meant a person who was non-intimidating, was still subordinate, and managed to make enough money to prove they were not monsters for slavery, but not enough to usurp their dominance.

Many would excel in this way. 200 years of slavery taught us how to follow directions. But nothing healed us. Nothing showed us how to mend our families. How to undo the idea that the worth of our men was in their physical strength and prowess like that of a prized Arabian horse. There wasn't a single resource to unteach women to grit and bear mistreatment or to feel "lucky" to have a man to take care of her. As if she hadn't been caring for multiple families and tending to her own master's children by herself. No one showed us the fallacy of what we had seen. We based "upstanding" relationships on what we saw at Massa's house. A Plantation owner who kept Black bodies as pets and lorded his will over their backs and in their sex and then allowed them to worship the same Christ he was so devoted to on Sundays. That was the model.

It's no wonder.

The brokenness. The fatherlessness. The misogyny. The myth of the good girl. The infidelity. The Church-going dysfunctionality was bred into us and then used to demean us. They beat us with a stick and laid it in our lifeless hands as they yelled, "Look what you have done to yourself!" Their pointed fingers and ridicule only made us strive harder to prove that we could be just like them. We could do what they do. We could have nuclear families and college degrees. In fact we did prove that. We did those things.

Lying broken in the midst of it all.

Watching the exchange between the Cool White Woman and the Graduate Professor forced me to critique myself. To play the cruel game of comparison where I try to decipher, down to our zodiac signs, what edge she might possibly have that allowed her to be heard and not me. Why she was intrinsically more reliable than I. The woman in my class was able to both argue the points she didn't feel valid and fully embrace the notes she agreed with. Certain moments felt defensive—a faux pas in the writing community, a sign you were too precious and unyielding—but it didn't feel wrong. It felt like passion and self-assurance. I had noted, before we even began the session, that she hung her jean jacket on the back of her chair and made sure there was no crease so that after our two-hour seminar she would leave as pristine as she had come in. That type of attention to detail felt like a hallmark of a reliable woman. Who wouldn't trust a person who thought enough about the future that she had the foresight to not lazily drape or stuff her jacket somewhere and regret it the rest of the day?

A portion of her piece, which was a story about her life, recounted her having almost pulled a gun on what she thought to be an intruder as a youth (it was her brother, who she hadn't known had snuck out of the house). Through her lens and recollection of events, this was proof that her childhood had been loving but quasi-abusive. She thoughtfully concluded through her work, via her life as a mother, that she would never allow a child to handle guns and teach them to shoot people at such a young age and she therefore was neglected. Most of our class agreed. I was scared to have an opinion.

Another woman in our class commented about how the portion of the story about guns made her cry. She was struck so deeply by the thought of what children in "less progressive parts of the country" endure. That woman was a nature writer. Her piece was barely critiqued, as commonly happened for writers of her genre. Outside of technical machinations and format, there isn't much. So few of us have input about blue herons or estuaries that as long as the work flows and seems vivid, we leave well enough alone. The professor was no different in his notes. While I did find some rather smart and his limited knowledge of the nature writer's subject impressive, his suggestions were limited to syntax and a "stronger opening paragraph." She was quintessential, if not stereotypical, as far as nature writers go. Long flowing gray hair that made you imagine her true age. The length and vibrancy of her bohemian clothing could have placed her in her forties. The grey and sun worn skin may have meant a vegan diet suited her and her sixties were kind. I always appreciated nature writers although I never understood their work. They know themselves and what matters to them most and dedicate their lives to writing about such things. I like when people know who they are.

Regardless of whether I could fully grasp (or cared to grasp) the scope of what was on the page, nature writers have always had a special gift that most other writers don't readily pick up on: nature writers are the people most uniquely equipped to translate nature into prose. Not nature in the outdoor/plant/ physical world sense. Nature as in characteristics. The basic essence of a thing. It's not lost on me that the two areas those writers are best at writing share a noun. They are intrinsically connected, both building blocks and cornerstones of the larger world. Every nature writer I have ever met commiserates that they are so often unread and the genre so difficult because only nature people care about nature. I always say, "Make it analogous to a love story and they'll read it. Everyone loves love stories."

That always seems to cheer them up, although we all know they will still barely be read. Sometimes, we need reminders that even unpopular voices are needed. I tried to keep that in mind in this place. Perhaps I needed to be more like her.

When the nature writer shared her concern for the children whose parents taught them to shoot, I was almost certain that it would spark debate. The professor's politics had leaked out in his reading of me being the unreliable narrator. He had mentioned "liberal agendas" and other dog whistles that placed him squarely in a different ideological group than me. While it hadn't offered any solace, it did offer insight and I was sure he would have a response for the nature writer.

Before he could speak another woman in class did. Also blonde (now in my recollection only me, the professor, and the nature writer were non-blonde, but she could have been before nature writing aged her), this woman fell into the same category as me: acts tough to prove a point. We came in together the same year and had begun to get to know each other a bit. She was friendly. She fashioned herself the outcast of our program (and kind of was) but more because she wanted to be than anything else. Her thoughts and beliefs were fairly conservative—a natural byproduct of her time in the armed forces—but she was a sweet spirit and kind and helpful. While she may not have agreed with everything our very progressive program stood for, she understood at the very least why they stood for it. Her angst came from hearing all day for a week at a time that people with her beliefs were dumb or cruel or [fill in the blank]. She was none of those things.

"I didn't read the gun passage that way at all," she retorted. I remember she looked at our professor and waited for his response. After hearing that I was an unreliable narrator for discussing racism, it seemed as though her views would be accepted in this room, but she needed approval first. She didn't want to offend. He nodded in agreement. Just like in my undergraduate course, where gangly twenty-somethings longed for the ability to rip Toni Morrison to shreds but never felt safe to do so until that day, the professor greenlit what would have otherwise been choked back, only quietly discussed over beers while everyone else was at lunch.

"What I gathered when I read that," she continued "was that you were a very responsible little girl. You knew and learned gun safety. You were a practiced marksman. You thought you were in danger and you did everything you were taught and used caution in your surroundings. I thought you were very brave."

"I agree with that," the professor chimed in.

I don't remember much of the response after that. There was one. I remember the writer's eyes widening at the thought that part of her story could have been perceived in such a way. I know the professor began talking again. My eyes had fallen back across him, against the white plaster. Under the fluorescent light. Beyond his ears again. To the textured wall. My thoughts jumbled and I took great pains to not take offense to what I was hearing. But it rolled from the gut into my chest. I imagined it much like a ball of gas or some earthen rupture that a nature writer might know about. There was a fundamental disagreement about perspective happening before me. There was a political disagreement about perspective happening before me. But nowhere in that disagreement on perspective were any of these women determined unreliable. She was not an unreliable narrator. The point of the gun was argued and discussed but never was her lens questioned. Never had she been told that an audience wouldn't trust her because she couldn't prove that parents allowing their children to learn shooting was dangerous. The professor's perspective (with his own set of facts) was that of responsible parenting. The Cool Writer's perspective (with her own personal experience and set of facts) was that it was reckless. He heard her and saw her point but disagreed. They moved on. The class moved on. I didn't. I couldn't.

> The millennial generation was the first to truly challenge the notions. Blame it on therapy. Blame it on the internet, who knows. But we were the first to challenge how it's always been. Not all of us. Not even most of us. But a significant minority explored the idea that everything as is was not the totality of what things could be. We began to search for our

healing. A healing that encompassed generations before us. That we have had to seek closure and understanding for our mothers and grandfathers and family without their permission or cooperation. We have had to be the first to, although quietly, find the fault in situations that previously went undiscussed and determine where we see ourselves in it. Do I think like that? Do I hold remnants of that mentality? Those ways? What can I do to not bring that into the generation after me?

The cross we bear is heavy but necessary to realize ourselves fully.

What was it about me that kept this experience in a sort of karmic cycle? The undeniable difference was my race. Me being a Black woman and all that comes with it. The consideration of race seemed too simple. I knew it was part of it. A large part of it. But there was more. I was born and raised in the South and had seen racism's many forms. I knew it to be overt, covert, passive aggressive, subtle. I knew Sunday morning racists and "I love the quarterback, but he can't date my daughter." This wasn't quite that. This was messier. More nuanced. I didn't feel smart enough to put my finger on it. I had enrolled in this program to feel smart enough. This was the professor who hated Morrison championing Baldwin because Baldwin is "undeniable." (He *is* undeniable, but the same could be argued of Morrison.) In this seminar, two unique, politically charged positions were taken. One was considered debatable. The other was fallacy. There was no matter of taste or difference in opinion. One lens was true, the other was not. One was good and one was bad. There was a common denominator in that both professors were white men. But the people who agreed with them varied as did the folks who disagreed. The only thing that seemed constant was that in both moments, the professor—the man who held the power—felt that he alone could make the determination as to what was true. Only they could decide.

I very suddenly understood. My eyes shifted from the wall to back to the professor's face. I made eye contact. I engaged again in the class. There were no points argued. If I heard and received the note he was giving the author I agreed. If I didn't, I scribbled my note in the margins of their work in hopes that they would read my perspective, whether it differed from both his and theirs or if I thought them correct. I saw, in that split second, that the problem wasn't me or us, it was them. If a fact or truth can shift based on the beliefs of the person holding it, then it cannot be a fact or truth. It is an opinion. While it may be true to the holder, it is not verifiable or objective. By their own standards, this professor and the professor before him were unreliable narrators. They were merely projecting onto me.

> The myth of the Good Girl exists in the only way that myths can: without further investigation. The Iliad is required reading for all young people and could easily be considered historic until we dig into history. Are their portions that could be true? Sure. Was Troy a real place? Some believe it may have been. But there is far more fallacy to it than proven fact. That is the Good Girl. The Good Girl is an epic poem that is beautiful and historic and tragic in that its sole purpose is to make us yearn for ways past that actually never existed. It's a tale of victories that never happened. Of obstacles that were never overcome. Of lives that were never lived. The Good Girl does not win.

The Good Girl was a natural response to freedom that was taken. It was a way to set some of us apart. To make us feel better, special, worthy in a world that treated us like nothing. In chattel slavery a Good Girl made her massa happy. It never brought her freedom. Post-slavery, a Good Girl made her husband happy—the husband who molded his role on the massa. It never brought her a happiness. Post-reconstruction, the Good Girl was the doting mother and devoted partner who kept her sexual partners low and her religious morals high. It never brought her love. But instead of abandoning the ideas of the "Good Girl," culture instead taught us to abandon the spoils of being one and be content. Freedom, happiness, and love were soon taught to be overrated and unnecessary to live a full life. Just be a Good Girl.

To this day no one can answer why.

Women with multiple sexual partners do get married. Women without degrees live prosperous lives. Children are raised and loved and thrive when their mother works outside of the home. Equality with their partners, communication, give and take, and egalitarianism in the home have actually proven to create stronger marriages, not weaker ones. Almost every aspect of the "Good Girl" mythology has been proven to be unfounded.

The goal of the narrator is to lead the reader through the story, guiding them through internal thoughts and offering perspective on backstory and future consequence. It is imperative that the reader trust the narrator (or otherwise know where their shortcomings are to adjust one's own perspective) and feel like what we are learning as we read is true. These professors—both white males—were unreliable. Their own perspectives on racism or womanhood—or anything—could never be reliable because their objectivity shifted whenever they felt the urge and there was no one to challenge their behavior. They proposed to place themselves on the top of the food chain. Our country told them since her inceptions that their perception was superior to others—their lens the most "logical"—and that their opinion matters most. Should they ever be physically or emotionally beaten down by a more dominant force, they were inherently led to believe that their phylum of folks, namely them, were higher on the food chain regardless. The only people who could possibly challenge such conjectures with any hope of movement were men like them. Considering men like them held no information whatsoever about women like me—outside of what they would read by our hand that they deemed unreliable—they had no information. Anything they projected onto us was faulty at best.

They never had to read books about us. Only the ones about men like them. My ideas of classics were all encompassing. Theirs were limited. Into my thirties I am still being introduced to classic works and classic literature and accept it all as truth. If they have never heard of it, you must qualify to them why it is a classic. I have been conditioned to understand that other voices matter and to reconcile them with my own because I know how it feels to be silenced. They talk the loudest, over everybody, and, with the single most limited perspective of any group, decide who is authentic and classic and well and right and true.

Unreliable narrators.

In that way, all of the rest of us are nature writers to them. A genre at the bookstore that should be there and has some good writers but is generally boring and only there to discuss the parts of life that are necessary and beautiful but niche. Most will never feel the need to pick up Zadie Smith any more than they will purchase a copy of the *Big Book of Sea Turtles*. Walden, however, will be on their mantle. It reminded me of Annie Dillard's "Total Eclipse." Prior to my program I had never heard of Annie Dillard. I was told by a professor and others that she was a great—a respected artist and purveyor of human nature. I read her based on that alone. People whom I respected relayed to me that in their world—nature writing—she was a great. Other literary figures seemed to agree. I could have given two shits about a solar eclipse. I read a new perspective because I respected the people who loved it and lived it. That was enough to be reliable to me.

At its worst, it was not boring. At its best, "Total Eclipse" was one of the best essays I had ever read. While I will never make the argument that all nature writers should write like Dillard, I will sort of make that argument because she allowed me, a Black woman who associates the outdoors with an assault on my hair, to see myself in nature. She described how the vastness of the total eclipse was so huge, so looming, that those watching let out audible gasps. Some inadvertently screamed. She couldn't tell the beginning and the end of darkness and for the moments of the eclipse said, "They got the world wrong." She felt like she knew this world but it wasn't the world it was supposed to be. Everyone she spoke to at the diner after the eclipse experienced a similar feeling: the smallness of our being, that they were somehow inconsequential in those moments. I knew those feelings. They were inherently mine. Dillard's recollection of the eclipse astutely described my feelings and the feelings of Black folks as a collective after witnessing yet another state sanctioned police shooting. Like a total eclipse, it is something we bear witness to because we should. We stand in front of it, purposefully, awkwardly, not knowing what to expect but bracing ourselves for something massive. A sight that will stay with us for decades. That we too will write about. Like the forthcoming shadow of the eclipse, we force ourselves to watch as the terror encompasses us, but we cannot look away. We mustn't. We knew what was coming when we determined to show up. To watch. We have to keep our eyes open. To say we saw it. Our discomfort grows audible—our fear, our grief. Like the darkness, it's infinite. We can't tell where any of it will begin or end and we ask ourselves for days upon days if the world is safe. Every millisecond of our lives we spent believing ourselves transcending some kind of racial barrier becomes pulverized with the rush of the darkness. We are lost in it. Reduced to it. We wonder if we got the world wrong. When we dine, or walk to the coffee shop, or go to work, or sit with our family we discuss how small we feel. Helpless. Our lives inconsequential.

The essay's most poignant section is when Dillard describes what came to her recollection that morning as she mulled over the event on her third cup of coffee. She wrote that she remembered seeing the cars on the hill just above the flat area where she was standing keep driving. A few pulled over for a moment, but then continued on their way, unphased and unaffected by the thing that made Dillard and so many others question their existence. How could that have happened?

Perspective. From that place, high on the hill above the plane where the droves came to watch the celestial phenomenon occur, the eclipse was not in full view. From their perspective in those cars—higher than everyone else—there was some darkness but not total. There wouldn't be a total eclipse at that exact angle for another hundred years. These drivers knew this event was taking place that day (traffic was horrible and employers in nearby Yakima allotted an extra hour for them to get to work in anticipation of the back-ups), but for whatever reason, seeing it for themselves was of no interest to them. Or maybe it was, but they couldn't get off work or miss school or that appointment. The cost of the other perspective was too great a risk to their status quo. Or future. Regardless, the folks who left that total eclipse left changed. For everyone on the hill a few miles away, this was another Monday morning. I would imagine that someone who had chosen that day to experience the eclipse for themselves might be hard to understand after such a life-changing event. It seemed to bring on an acute existential crisis for everyone who watched it from the Yakima bank. Collectively experiencing that crisis would feel comforting. Trying to explain the depth and breadth of a newfound panic—one that came as a result of having watched the entire world go dark—was probably not easily understandable to anyone who chose to stay on the hill. It was probably annoying to them. Overblown. Fantastic. Same world, same place, same access to varying perspectives, and still, those that didn't experience the eclipse would never be able to share in that space. Unless they read Dillard. But no one reads nature writers.

What we have found is that empowering a woman is scary. Even for other women. A woman with too many ideas, too much will, and too much intelligence is dangerous because she questions how things are. She forces the hard answers. Many of those answers would make us have to do the hard work of healing a break that has already set improperly. Meaning we would have to break it again for it to be set correctly and to heal well. We vehemently fight that work because the reward doesn't seem to warrant the pain.

But it does. Freedom is always worth the pain.

The unreliable narrators in my life missed total eclipses. They never saw acts of God or human travesty in quite the same way as those who were forced to experience it. That's not to say they never saw a lunar eclipse or storms or problems. But the all-encompassing change was so foreign to them that they considered their "version" everyone's version and our stories seemed "too this" or "too that" because it didn't match theirs. These men were told they were the gatekeepers to truth. Everyone else was wrong. Every child in America knowing *A Farewell To Arms* and believing alcoholic veterans who womanize a sympathetic byproduct of war that they will never see, but questioning the "personal responsibility" of Black and brown veterans who came home with the same afflictions and vices and were met with hostility and kept from opportunity. They will never see the jumbled disparity. Totally unreliable.

Years later, as I prepared for graduation and my final manuscript, I chose to write specifically about who determines authenticity for writers of color. I shared this story with one of my professors. She was astounded that I had gone through that my very first course of my program.

"I'm so sorry that happened, Vanessa."

"It's okay, it was a long time ago."

"I'm surprised you didn't quit the program."

I thought about that. I had quit before for a lesser infraction. This time was different.

"It helped me." I told her, "It helped me see that my voice doesn't have to be the same or even liked by someone who is committed to misunderstanding. It matters."

I didn't mention it also made me start reading nature writers.

FIVE

MIRACLE OF BLACK LOVE

Tonight, as my ex-husband left my house, we laughed about something. I don't remember the joke. He rolled the blue plastic hamper out of my door—the same hamper that had been in our shared bathroom when we were married, now filled with clothes from his one-bedroom, appliance-less apartment—and reminded me to lock the door when he left.

"I'll see you tomorrow," he said, still laughing.

I never would have thought, almost a decade ago, that this would be our nightly routine. Dinner. Bath time. Bedtime stories and prayers. Then retreating to separate corners of a 1200-square-foot condo to regroup from the day, debrief for the next, and be off. Our wedding didn't feel that long ago. It had been five years when I left him. It was now a month shy of seven. I used to have to remind him of the date. Now I only remember the year. Occasionally the month. Almost a decade of my life—a blur of happiness, brokenness, joy, and grief. New beginnings. Painful endings. I stood at my kitchen island, hands firmly placed on the cedar, and forced myself to breathe.

To look around my home. My home. The home that I love and made my own. That I chose. That I worked hard for. A home that did not include him.

I locked the door. Whatever the very funny joke was, it was made even sweeter by the fact that we had enjoyed it together. In my home.

* * *

No one intends on getting divorced when they get married. I've heard some say that they "kind of knew it wouldn't last" but even those people I don't believe. I think they knew this union probably wouldn't work but hoped beyond hope for a miracle. That process of thinking is nowhere near as nonsensical as some would have you believe.

To maintain a marriage requires miracles. Anyone who chooses to get married is believing in that miracle. Two humans—raised differently, from different backgrounds and different parts of the country (or at least different addresses), with different thoughts, needs, and wants—deciding that they will hang out with each other forever is supernatural. Most of us never even want to hang out with ourselves that long. For two people who, no matter their age, are ever evolving on a timeline not their own, promising to grow together until they die is a great act of faith. Not knowing if it will work and choosing to do it anyway may be *the* hallmark of those of us with the most faith. I believed in the miracle.

We see it every day. High school sweethearts. College loves. Second, third, fifth marriages that ended up lasting when the others couldn't. Partnerships which never wanted or were perhaps denied the official title of marriage yet determined for themselves to uphold similar tenets. These people vowed to make a life and home together, regardless of the cost. In the home of one of my childhood best friends, his mother had stenciled above the marital bed, "As long as we don't give up on the same day." The wall was robin's egg blue. The words were shiny and reflected the deep brown of the stencil in the light above their bed. Every morning they would have to wake and face that mantra in the same hue as their cocoa-brown skin. It's as if they removed the stencil from their own bodies and plastered it to the wall as a blood oath. Both on second marriages. Married to this day. They purposed to never forget the work behind the miracle.

I thought I had, too.

Early in my separation, I wondered where we had made our misstep. When I saw the first text come through on my ex's iWatch, which he had accidentally left on the black granite kitchen counter, I was confused. When I saw his real time response, I laid the watch gently back down and walked to the stairs where I promptly sat. The stairs were lined with a white and grey Moroccan runner that I had dutifully laid myself only a few months earlier when we moved into that townhome. Our two-year-old toddled up and down those stairs and the runner was meant to break a fall. I sat there. I did not cry. I called no one. I sat, winded. I exhaled and looked out of the window from my place on the lowest step. I had hung those curtains. It was gorgeous outside. We had moved in because of this exact scenery.

Months prior, we lived upstairs in the unit right above. When we moved to Glendale, we were taking a huge leap.

Our rent was $800 more than it had been in South Los Angeles. We had a baby, and daycare costs. We had to get a second car. But we were also making more money. Our careers were both finally in the places we had toiled so long for. We hired movers (something we had never had the means to do before and considered a white person's luxury). We financed furniture—stuff we actually liked, not just what we could afford. I kept my anxiety at bay the entire move-in day. I worried about finances. About doing too much too fast. About living in Glendale.

When everything was settled and we looked around at this gorgeous new condo with grass and neighbors and play-grounds, I jumped up and down like a child into his arms. I had never dreamed we could do this. There were moments—long moments—this never seemed possible. We would watch our white counterparts in the film and television and music industry, with new cars and decent housing and we would wonder what kind of money they must come from. Neither of us came from poverty, but our parents couldn't be quite that safety net. Our safety was a soft place to land back home should this not work in Los Angeles. Not a lifeline. Every Black person we knew in LA struggled like that. We all had that conversation. When we found ourselves parents, we decided we wanted to offer our son that lifeline one day. Struggle is great and character-building but freedom to create and not worry about survival seemed better. So we got busy. We worked harder, longer, and more dutifully then anyone I knew. Several jobs. People would comment on how much we worked. That afforded us this place. We promised each other we would never, ever, be late on rent here. Or on any bills for that matter. We were creating our miracle, for him and for us.

Rent was never late. We had a few tight months. One month we had to take out a personal loan. I remember meticulously combing through the budget and not finding where our leak was. I assumed I wasn't paying close enough attention. One month, things were so tight we pawned my engagement ring to make the rent. I didn't care that much. After my son was born my fingers were never slim enough to wear it again, but it also didn't matter because we had each other's initials tattooed on our fingers. When we walked into the pawn shop in Glendale we spoke to the man behind the counter for a good while. I think we were both scared to pull the trigger. He learned about my family being from Seychelles. RJ traveling the world with pop superstars. We gave each other recs for restaurants. And then we pulled out my ring. He looked at us with a gaze I will never forget.

"Why do you want to get rid of this?"

The owner of the pawn shop either thought we were full of shit or perhaps had a drug problem. It didn't matter. His job was to do his job. We got about $400 for that ring. I would spend the next four years dodging questions about why I never wore it. My grandma would ask me all the time to put it on and I would brush her off as antiquated. She was. I had stopped wearing it long before we pawned it. I also didn't have it. The day it was sold, I remember watching RJ sheepishly walk back to our mint green Prius. We climbed in. Just enough to make the rent check before picking up our son at daycare.

"I'll get you another one, one day. It'll be better."

I knew that wasn't true. I can't explain how I knew it, but I did. I didn't think it was because we would divorce. I thought it was because I would never care enough to wear the damn ring to bother asking for another, and I knew him to be too flighty to ever think about it again without my asking. It seemed like such a small sacrifice. When people would hear the story later, they would gasp at my nonchalance. They thought me underplaying my feelings. That wasn't the case. I was working towards something bigger than the presentation of marriage. I was working for the miracle. I was attempting to give my Black son something that we didn't have. In my summation, a ring had little to do with that.

The next two years were great for work, finances, and family life. We had finally caught our stride, we were working towards our goals, and everything we had ever wanted seemed so close we could taste it. We were the Black family we had dreamed about it. That society told us didn't exist. That we wished we had growing up. That people applauded us for. Our little nuclear unit was a beacon of hope. We were our ancestors' wildest dreams. I checked real estate listings every night. We took vacations. We rarely ever fought and when we did it was about the workload of the house or his absentmindedness. Typical marriage. A far cry from the plights our families had when we were younger. Neither of us had the ability to stay mad for long and both of us had grown up in homes where the silent treatment and weeks of a parent being mad made home sometimes feel unbearable. We hated it. That was another thing we purposed our son would never have to deal with, so it just never happened. We would talk ad nauseum in one sitting, figure out our stuff, and keep it pushing. When the townhouse downstairs became available, we waited our landlord out to get the price of the rent where we wanted it and have him agree that he would allow part of our rent to go towards the purchase of the unit after a year. It took months, but we made the deal.

And here we were. Creating the miracle.

The day I sat on those stairs we were nine months in. Our son was almost three. RJ left his watch rushing out the door to take him to preschool. I could see his lunch box on the counter. I could feel the low pile of the runner under my hands. It was harder than the website had portrayed. My kid had some rug burns from it. Now I was rubbing my hands across it quickly, to gain friction and feel heat. My hands were freezing. I looked at the rugs in our kitchen. Those were fairly new. I took my time with each room, designing it and stalking various places for price cuts and reductions. I looked at our living room. A basket of toys. The couch we now owned. The dining room had our rustic eight-seat wooden-beamed dining table. We got that in South LA. We needed something for the house we were renting, and RJ was intent on that specific table. I thought he was crazy because it was $700. Almost half our rent and way too much for a dining room table. He insisted.

"We have to get into the habit of getting things we like and making a way."

It took us a year to pay it off. But we did it. And it was the beginning of us realizing that the world was bigger than we knew it to be. Everything wasn't about struggle or being behind the curve on what white people already had. We could do that too. We could have the American Dream. We could have everything they denied us.

I gazed at everything in the townhouse. I had a story for every square inch. I knew in that exact moment that all those stories were stories of my failed marriage.

* * *

FOR MANY OF US WHO GROW up Black—African American or otherwise—we grow up seeing a version of love exemplified on TVs and movie screens that looked nothing like the love of our homes. For those of us who were lucky enough to have a nuclear family—and by nuclear I only mean two loving parents, marital status or gender need not qualify that—few saw the affectionate, flower-baring sentimentality that Hollywood told us was the ideal love. The best of us saw commitment. Duty. Loyalty. Special birthday dinners and hand-holding on the couch watching favorite programs at night. Those of us lucky enough to have parents or family who we deemed "couple goals" marveled at sporadic date nights and cruises to the Bahamas. We dreamed of a love like that. Dancing at weddings. Christmas gifts. Adorably jumbled attempts at anniversaries. That looked great.

Most didn't see that. If we were so lucky to have had two parents in our home, they were plagued with the weight of being Black in America. Raising Black kids in America. Surviving. They worked tediously. Whether middle class or working poor, there was always a quiet hum of "who gon' pay for that?" below the surface. Some fortunate enough to be "well off" would keep that hum—though possibly quieter—always faced with the stark reality that the privilege they had was built on quicksand. At any given moment it could all fall apart or be taken away. As children, we grew up seeing that. Sometimes we idolized it. Sometimes we wanted to do the entire opposite of what we saw. But the most central theme I have seen through my own life and those around me is that whichever we chose, we were never sure which was "right."

Love for the sake of love had been something long denied Black relationships. Slavery decimated Black marriage. Even if a slave held it sacred, your body was not your own. You could be used to father or mother dozens of children, removed from their upbringing and your chosen spouse, and bred again. Even there, what was love? That's not to take away from the resiliency of the human spirit or the transcendence of intimacy and shared values and beliefs, but when in bondage what is desirable? Is it someone's ability to endure abuse? Protect from abuse? To labor so as to be favored by your master? When a people is relegated to their output, who then becomes valuable? What is valuable? It's not the thinker or the painter. The ability to wipe away tears or make someone laugh or feel wanted might be nice, but it is not a hallmark of "good." It's a bonus. Pass that down through sharecropping, then Jim Crow, then a crack epidemic, all the while being racially and economically discriminated against and our love—Black love in America—has never really had a chance to blossom at its foundations. For the survival of ourselves and each other it has traditionally been about caretaking and togetherness and two people's ability to rise above a station together. At the very least to be able to live together. It's still been beautiful. But it has been robbed the chance to go as deep as freedom would allow it.

Through progress and the freedom of youth, young people are where we see Black love in its purest form. I would watch in high school as the white boys would court their white girl-friends. They were always so desperately in love. Several young white boys in my area tragically took their own lives in my teenage years because of heartbreak. It seemed crazy to me for them to love their girlfriends that much. Heartbreak was reserved for women. Growing up at my grandma's, I saw my uncles and cousins get their feelings hurt. If they ever cried it was over death. Or competition. Sometimes anger. All those feelings were acceptable reasons for men to shed tears. And our family was "progressive" in that way. I never heard that boys shouldn't cry. We laughed at my grandpa all the time because he cried every first day of school, first step, first Easter speech . . . he cried at all our milestones. I never saw anyone cry over a woman.

The white boys made no sense to me. For all the talk of white superiority, they always seemed so weak. The way they would wait for their girlfriends outside of their classes or hold them around the waist at every moment as though, should they not be tethered together for even a second, she might float away. Black parents like my own would scoff at those white kids. It was so inappropriate for children to be demonstrating such acts of affection. They were fast. That's how people got pregnant.

Then I fell in love.

I felt so special when my boyfriend would do those things. I would constantly be in trouble for being up until the wee hours of the morning, sneaking to talk to him on landline phones, head under pillows until a parent picked up in the middle of the night and said "Go to bed!" The dread I would feel having to face an adult the next morning was not enough to stop it from happening again, because the feeling of being loved was all-encompassing. The feeling of a boy holding your hand or holding your *anything* in public felt like such acknowledgement. He wanted his friends to see. He wanted it to be known that the two of you loved each other. That *he* loved *you*. There was no burden of providing or jobs or children or society. It was Black love. Beautifully unadulterated by the world. Maybe the only time in many of our lives we would ever be able to just love without the weight of "how will it work." I wanted that. My girlfriends wanted that.

We learned early to not dare *expect* it. Black men were not supposed to do that. They were supposed to keep it cool at all times, perpetually unbothered unless someone was trying to "steal you." No one's parents should see too much affection because you weren't being sent to school for that. Too much thought about significant others meant too little thought about academics or sports. You had a lifetime for the "problems" of relationships as adults had come to know it. The thing that could get you the furthest ahead in life, that could separate you from struggle, was your output. Your career. Your future. When you were stable and could provide then you were in a place to "find love"—find someone who was "equally yoked." Who was on your financial, societal, and spiritual level. Love was about teaming up for survival and there was no way you could know how to do that at sixteen. So little Black girls like myself dreamed of a love they were taught was not love but "feelings" and those two things were different. If we had a "good guy," we learned to accept what we got emotionally.

It wasn't just the little Black girls who suffered. I remember watching white boys discuss relationships in depth with their friends at lunch tables or in the back of geometry classes. They would give each other advice on women. Whatever that meant for sixteen-year-olds. Elaborate homecoming and prom asks. Two of my best friends were Black boys. We had grown up together since we were in elementary school. When they needed advice, they called me.

"What did your boys say when you asked them?"

"We don't talk about this kind of stuff. That's what girls are for." They knew then that emotions were for women. They had them. Needed to discuss them. Needed reassurance. Needed a hug. But they knew who to come to and who to wear a poker face around.

By senior year, most of the Black boys I knew had learned enough from teammates and older friends and barbershops to internalize that a "good" Black woman would be your ride-or-die. She would stand by you come hell or high water. The only requisite was that you privately give her the things the white boys did in public. She wouldn't ask for more. She knew. And in exchange she would take care of you. Cater to your needs. Give you sex.

With so little to have to give in return, it was wholly possible to collect women. To have needs met at any whim. Without the freedom to publicly display your love (or have it frowned upon or looked at as weak) there was a love deficit. Young Black men were looking for validation. Someone to loudly yell, "I love you," all the time. The world wouldn't give it to them. Their fathers were taught to mildly pat them on the back when they achieved something. The girls they loved were told to be quiet about their admiration. They were searching. And they'd get it wherever they could. Multiple people in a day if that's what it took. And somehow that seemed right.

The goal for all of us—Black men and women—was to have a stable family. To regain what we lost. To provide our children a solid foundation of love (as we saw it), care, resources, and guidance. To reclaim. That meant that we had to marry. We had to stay married. Black girls were taught to be wary of each other with boyfriends. We were all fighting for the same thing. We were taught to be even more weary of white girls who seemed to have no code and were not even thinking about long-term relationships. They were fine with just "hooking up." We didn't have that freedom. A white girl was allowed to explore love and sex and feelings and fun. Not us. To ever "amount to anything" we had to be on a laser-focused path of career, finances, and upstanding moral value. We had to show ourselves better than the next woman so a Black man would pick us to raise his family with. Everyone still hooked up all the time, but it could not be openly discussed because it lowered a Black woman's marital value. If several Black men "had" a woman, could you count on her to be loyal? Was she not serious about presenting well? White girls didn't have that worry. Black men didn't hold them to it either. How many people a white woman sleeps with isn't a mark against her because her worth is not in what she does. It's in her person. *We* had to be smart, and pretty, and educated. And have something going for us: our own car, our own money, a good relationship with our mama, our hair done—the list was endless—for us to be "wifey material."

All a Black man had to do was show up with at least a veiled readiness to create the miracle of living life together. He would try all the girls, desperate attempts to feel like someone who was loved. While we desperately attempted to prove ourselves worthy of love.

When things got serious with Black men in college and grad school, I remembered a few boyfriends calling their fathers. All but two of the men I dated had close relationships with their parents. I remember their fathers offering advice when I was angry: flowers or dinner or heart-felt apologies. The stuff I saw white boys doing when we were fourteen were the adult last-ditch efforts. That was evidence of their love. I remember one young man's father telling me on a weekend I went home with him that he knew his son loved me because he had never seen him so worried about losing a girl.

"A lot of young ladies came through this house. He would barely pay them attention. We knew this was different because he talked about you to us. When y'all had your little falling out, he was hurt. I knew he was. I could see it on his face. I told him 'If a girl can make you feel sad because she's sad . . . she might be the one.'"

That felt like such a compliment. His parents knew about me. He discussed me. He felt bad for being mean to me. The gravel-high bar for Black love was never questioned when I was that age. Often, it's not questioned now. Black men have had such little freedom to love and feel and *be* in our world that it is not necessary for them to totally feel it to engage. Rather "love" is transactional. I give you my care/attention/acknowledgement for your commitment to my needs. Needs that he is constantly being kept from being able to meet himself by virtue of the country we live in. Black women could always care for themselves and others. We are how Black men survived since infanthood. What we lacked is love, adoration, loyalty. Much like our brothers who looked to us to hold them down, we looked to them to hold us up. We've known Black man our whole lives. We know them capable of what the world keeps from them. The transaction seems fair: I can help you to wholeness while you love me to wholeness. Together this whole unit will create whole children.

I've only now learned it doesn't work like that.

Love is not transactional. Love is so much deeper and more expansive than a single action or feeling. It is transformative. It changes how we view ourselves and others. You cannot love someone into a thing—we can't be loved into wholeness or fullness or greatness—instead someone loves us on our cellular level. That love empowers us enough to spring forth into new and evolved versions of ourselves. To have the freedom to be who we are fully and grow in that day by day. Year by year. In that love we never fear retribution or being dismissed for discovering ourselves because someone knows us deeply, sees us intimately and thinks we are wonderful. In that way love is freedom. That freedom allows children the safety to try a new sport or poorly play piano. That freedom allows a teen to pick a college far from home, or decide not to go at all and forge a new trail. It gives adults the steadfastness to quit a job. Or change their hair. And it is all predicated on knowing that you are loved and accepted regardless of how it goes. Whether you fail or succeed. Black folks were robbed of that the moment we were brought to these soils. Everything is about what we can do. What we can give. What we can show. Even our love.

They stole our miracle.

* * *

WHEN I MOVED TO LOS ANGELES, I lived with family friends. Their permanent home was in the Inland Empire, but they had a condo near Downtown Los Angeles that they would stay in from time to time to lessen commutes and when their kids had auditions. I lived in their spare room. They had furnished it for me with dressers and a futon from Ikea. Two years in, I moved into my first apartment in North Hollywood. It was 2011 and the rent was $800 for 700 square feet. The neighborhood was mostly working-class Latino. My grocery store, bank, and general services were in both Spanish and English. It felt like Florida. I was right at home.

I had met my ex-husband a few months before and we were casually dating. I wasn't sure where it was going but I knew I wasn't going to wait too long to find out. He was a traveling musician—who also played at the church where I met him—and frankly, he wasn't my type. He was short. Quirky. A Midwesterner through and through. He poured sugar on white rice and had never eaten a plantain. He owned exactly zero books—except the Bible—and had read negative four. He was possibly the nicest person I had ever met, which was also annoying because no one allowed for getting mad at him without wondering first if I had done something. He was too nice to be mad at.

The boyfriend before him had completely devastated me. There had been men in-between—all very nice, but nothing worth mentioning. I was having the most fun I had ever experienced in my twenty-five-year-old life without a man. The same friend whose parents had the stenciled marriage quote above their beds had told me years earlier "If you could leave dudes alone long enough, you would be dangerous." It took me time, but I eventually understood what he had tried to impart years earlier, as we sat on the warm pavement of my grandma's driveway while he consoled me through another broken relationship. Los Angeles was new. I was creating things. Working my way into a new industry and space. Men could wait. This time was for me. By not dedicating my time to providing for another man—giving fully of myself to prove worthy of relationship—I was using that energy for my own goals. For me. It was powerful.

My ex-husband's appearance in my life seemed different than the people before him. I had never dated anyone like him. In fact, my first few years in Los Angeles I wondered if I would meet anyone like *me*. I would later. The feeling that everyone was so different had everything to do with the social circle of transplants in big cities. Life in LA is like giant Double Dutch ropes, swinging quickly and alternating side-to-side. The buzz of the ropes whirling past your head, knocking you off-kilter and scaring you half to death with each repeated swing before you learn that this appealing game is actually dangerous and you should step back before you jump in. When you first move here, and maybe to any big city, you've only ever skipped rope. You've never seen anyone be able to rush multiple bands, jump in with such precision, dance through it, and jump out unscathed. It seems like a circus act that you have to have some special skill or ability to be able to do yourself. So you wait on the sidelines and watch others do it. Some with ease. Some get bonked on the head and the rope slows only enough for them to exit, hurt, and then picks up the pace again. You bob your head, trying to pick up on the timing that the successful ones somehow see. But it's terrifying. It seems impossible. You learn to make friends with the other people on the sidelines. You probably have nothing in common with them in real life, but here the most important thing is shared and that is that you are new and scared shitless of those damn ropes.

I wanted to jump in desperately. I wanted to learn how to do it. But after some time I had made such good friends with the people on the sidelines, I got stuck between the two worlds. In my little apartment, I worked diligently to figure out the pattern I needed to learn to get in the game. I had friends from Florida who did the same. But outwardly, I went to church. I hung with people there and extensions of them, most all transplants who had come for the same reason as me. Some had been waiting to jump in a decade longer than I had and felt they had tried everything, and it simply didn't work. You had to know somebody who could already jump. You had to be gifted with special skills to jump. You had to come from money so your parents could have hired a teacher to show you how to jump. I was taking it all in, and still something inside me told me I could figure it out. When I met my ex, he was on the other side of the ropes. I watched him get hit by them sometimes. Sometimes make it in and be able to get a few good jumps in before rushing out, panting. And then he'd do it again. Better each time. I appreciated that. So did the people at our church. He was one of the few exceptions that everyone saw as being both like us and different. They saw him as "blessed." I saw him as unafraid. In that way, we were alike. Even though neither of us were fully Double Dutching yet, we knew we didn't want to stay on the sidelines anymore and we were going to figure it out. My method was calculated. Watching. Learning measured attempts. His was balls to the wall. If you get hurt, put some ice on it and try again. He gave me courage to go for it more often. I made him wait and watch before jumping into things blindly. Together we could conquer these ropes. It never dawned on us that, just like everyone else, our commonality first started by meeting on the sidelines. He felt like me. He felt like people from Florida. He felt like home.

I collected pieces of home. My one-bedroom apartment quickly became a hostel, brimming with people who were an extension of Florida or my college years or something that wasn't the sidelines. It was helpful to have multiple people pitching in on the rent. I was also raised to not let people "out on the street." If you need a place to lay your head, lay it here. My childhood friend, Greg, lived on the Ikea futon I brought with me from the spare room I first lived in. He was from Orlando and we had done TV shows together when we were younger. Our families always stayed in touch and we did, too, sporadically through social media. He was short but not small framed. The darkest, smoothest skin I had ever known. He frequently cleaned his face with Sea Breeze and that smell wafted throughout the small apartment whenever he was home.

A woman from church, Roberta, shared my bed with me a ton. She was my age and from Miami. A dramaturg. We had a few mutual friends from Florida theater. Roberta had locs down her back that she maintained beautifully. She had lived a hundred lives, from Shakespearian theater in Oregon to blue-collar Pittsburgh. I remember looking at her reading *Americanah* by Chimamanda Ngozi Adichie and drinking wine on my floor one day. Wondering how she was so mature. No one at church did things like that. They were often too scared to have a glass of wine, not because they were worried drinking was a "sin" but because that was the behavior of the people in the Double Dutch ropes and they had not yet successfully integrated into that life. Even though they wanted so badly to be there, a lot of times they would turn their noses up at anything people in those ropes did. It helped them, I think, to try and convince themselves that the sidelines were preferable. That way they wouldn't be so sad if they never figured out how to jump in. They hated Roberta for that. For feeling free enough to do whatever the hell she wanted to do. They masked it as other things, but it was jealousy of her freedom and her refusal to act like them. She had no regard for their opinions or their attempts at looking like they had it all together. She was tough and dramatic and self-involved. But she was smart, and courageous, and exactly who she is and that's what they hated the most.

Josh was the baby of the hostel and he slept on the floor in the living room. He was like a little brother. He reminded me of mine. I met him doing a play in LA after his parents had "kicked him out." In truth they wanted him to get his shit together and he didn't want to and so was sleeping in his truck. His mother had been like an aunt to me since I moved to California and I quietly told her he could stay with me until we convinced him to move back home. He never did, but he did reconcile with his family and get his own place. Once, we went to a big birthday celebration for his mother at their home, which I had never visited. We drove onto an estate in Chatsworth. A tennis court. A huge pool. Open fields. His mother laughed; his antics were always of petulance. I cursed him out that night.

There was also an ever-revolving door of occupants. One of my best friends from Florida, Dana, stayed for a while as she tried to figure out if she wanted to move to LA and pursue makeup. Tre, one of my dear friends who was a music producer in Atlanta would stay whenever he had sessions in Los Angeles. People who were displaced. Depressed. Just wanted good company or good food. They were always at my house. We never fought over the one bathroom. Or cereal. Or anything. To consider so many grown people literally sleeping in every corner may seem chaotic. It never was. It was fun. And it was eye opening. It lead us to some of our deepest and most intimate experiences of life. We came to love each other. To know each other's desires and pursuits and to hold one another up as we tried to become the people we had to be to reach our goals.

We would stay up, my ex often amongst us, until all hours of the night, talking about our dreams for the future. He would always engage. But he would always go home. He would come for the fellowship and food and then leave. I didn't mind that. He had his own home with his own bed with not nearly as many people. When I would start to stay at his house more, he opened up to me about not liking my living situation. I told him I was helping friends. They were helping with rent. And I loved the companionship and what it was teaching me about myself, my work, the industry. I loved exploring the city with people. I grew up like this, too.

"I didn't. My family would never have let anything like that happen. We don't really do friends like that. We have them, but your family is your friends. I do things with my cousins. That's all a little much for me."

We weren't deep enough in dating for this to be deal breaker. We were at the stage where we were deciding if this is the person I *should* date. I told him my little apartment wasn't going to change but I was glad he told me. We were just different. Plus, he wasn't going to pay my rent. He had a very decent paying gig with a well-known musician. He wasn't rich but he wasn't struggling like me. He kept jumping in the ropes. I needed to watch these people and others a little longer to figure out how to do that for myself. He'd always come back. The next day. And the next. And the next. He opened up more. Tried new foods. Went on adventures. But always insisted he stay the night at his house. That seemed like a fair compromise.

I can't remember now how the dynamic changed. Or how long it took. But soon, without the community, he became the person I was most focused on. And soon, without being forced to open up to more people or try more things or learn different ways, he became closed off to the idea of needing that anymore. We could jump in the ropes together as planned and maybe we didn't need to study anyone. Maybe we could simply take our bonks on the head with grace and try again without help. It was better that way, after all. No one could hold your mistakes against you. I never agreed with that. I had learned from the hostel and from life that watching and learning were equally as important as doing. That loving and being with other people created a safe place for us to watch and learn. I had seen it! So had he! But our Black love programming took over. Our determination to be a thing—to jump inside those ropes and be able to jump in and out as though we belonged—made us cower to one another. I separated from the hostel, leaving it weeks on end without stepping foot inside. Not seeing my friends. I was on the outside of what they were doing, unable to learn from them. He started going harder with his jump attempts. If he asked me to focus on this and abandon that, now he would have to provide. He had to figure this out. His house became my house although none of my things were there. There was no real space for my clothes or stuff. I was transient yet permanent. We settled into the Black love we had always known. Transactional. I gave him this he gave me that and together we could get somewhere.

We successfully jumped in and left the sidelines behind. He pulled me in after him. I didn't learn then to jump myself. Instead, the new vision was I take care of him and he jumps for the both of us. It was all we knew, and in LA we only knew each other.

* * *

THE SAFER AT HOME ORDER FOR Los Angeles County came the second week of March 2020. I wasn't concerned about it. I was gainfully employed and would be throughout the summer. If my calculations were correct, I could hold out the entire year if I needed to. If I got another job, even better. At that point, we didn't think we would be holding an entire year. Or even two months. In retrospect, I don't know what we thought. I just know we didn't think we'd be locked away so long.

My ex had just moved to his one-bedroom apartment two-and-a-half miles from my condo in Larchmont Village. I had made the decision six months prior to leave Glendale. When we divorced, he asked me to stay close so that he could see our son regularly and I had. I leased an apartment walking distance from our old townhouse. I bought a cheap couch and dinette. TVs. A bed for my room. A shelf for my books. I decided to figure everything else out as I went. The only room I did everything for upon move-in was my son's room. I was so fearful that he would feel displaced. That the little boy who literally adored sleeping, sitting, hugging between his mommy and daddy was going to feel so uncertain about a new house and new room where his father was not present. I wanted everything perfect. I bought him a new bed with the exact same set he had at the old house. Wallpaper. Rugs. A toy box full of new toys. I didn't want him to feel like we robbed him of his miracle. He never seemed to stutter-step. His transition made mine so much easier.

The same could not be said for my ex. Prior to my leaving him, he had decided to try and focus on music directing instead of touring. Our son was getting older and he wanted to be home more often. Until you make a name for yourself in music directing, work can be sporadic. Sparse checks were of no consequence in a two-income home—especially with my new television writer's income—but then our lives were blown apart. In the midst of relationship turmoil, he never paused to consider the financial ramifications of our split. He had never thought about how our love worked because of my sacrifice. Although our lives looked so different, he still considered our love in the way he considered the loves we saw growing up.

He never conceded the fact that we would not get back together. He still has never verbally conceded that, although I'm sure we both know and often talk about second marriages now. He had witnessed the miracle of marriage through his own family. There were moments like this. But nothing ever ended. It couldn't. The goal was an intact family and so women long suffered. I had seen the same. What's more, most women couldn't afford to take care of their children or themselves when things went awry. So they looked inward. What more could they do or should they have done to make their relationship work. We grew up in households that read the Bible regularly, and women were often told to be a Proverbs 31 women. Be everything. He knew that was the type of woman I wanted to be. That was my goal too. That's why we were here. That is why we had come so far. There was no possible way that we would truly ever split because this was par for the course.

Watching those traditional, slavery-founded family structures leads Black men to sometimes feel entitled to a woman's all when they are only giving their "some." If I complained about having too much on my shoulders, I would sometimes get reprimanded by friends about treating him like a "kid" and taking care of too much for him and around our home. My pain was my fault. Let him fall. Let him grow up. Let him be a man. Then, when I would refuse to remind him to pay the bills or generally be an adult and the lights were cut from lack of payment or the IRS was breathing down our necks, the same people would tell me to "learn each other's strengths and weaknesses and help him learn." It was always my job to sacrifice. He wasn't (and isn't) a bad person or just an irresponsible man. He was the product of Black love.

When I left, that job of fixing and responsibility became his own, and he had no clue how to even identify what he should do first. I wasn't there to solve it. He had spent so long allowing himself to believe that when I complained about him "doing more" I was "doing too much." My own family would sometimes remind me that he worked so hard. That he had carried us into the ropes. It didn't matter that I had wanted to learn to do that too. That I *was* doing that too. He *did* it. The least I could do was hold down the fort. It drove me to repeat my earliest years in Los Angeles. Outwardly, do all the things a good wife does, but quietly study the ropes again, so I could jump in for myself. Eventually, I jumped in with him on my own volition and never stopped holding it down. I was Proverbs 31 incarnate. I was a Pinterest mom at home while busting ass in my career. I was all things to all people. Except myself. Even then I would get bombarded with whispers of better physical appearance. Lose weight. Do more to my hair. Be sexier. Do everything possible to make him happy. I was exhausted and dying and did not know it because it was the exact model I had seen, and I was doing it better than even them.

When we broke up, I was the only one of us that could both care for myself and work. He didn't know how to do even the slightest bit of saving or cooking or planning. My first year after separation, albeit emotionally difficult, was one of the best of my life. It was the opposite for him. Everything we had built crumbled because it had been built on my back, a back that was now standing erect.

While he became more despondent and in need of work, I carried the brunt of caring for our child. The commute from Glendale to my job and school every day was taxing—especially when my ex was able to help less and less due to less income and needing to take gigs wherever he could. I gave him a few months' notice after a particularly long run of single parenting and told him I was moving into LA proper. I needed a closer commute. I needed more help. And I wanted to live somewhere of my own choosing. A community that represented my values, that was about what I liked, and was encompassing of where I was going and not where we were. I was full swing in the ropes. He was on the sidelines again. I wasn't going to sit with him. He had made me sit down so long.

Money was tight but he insisted on moving too. A new start would be good for him, letting go of the townhouse that was now too expensive. The space that held all kinds of memories. The stairs with the Moroccan runner. The $700 table. He even told me he threw out our Christmas tree. He couldn't bear putting it up without me. It was a tinsel-covered reminder of what used to be home.

The move was hard for him financially. The first day I walked in to pick up Ryder, I was so put off by the puke green carpet that lined the hallways to his new apartment, I never looked up. I followed it, like a brick road leading to a dungeon. Everything smelled earthy, as if we were underground. The number of his apartment was crooked. I considered straightening it before I knocked but resigned to letting well enough alone.

When I walked in, our son was jumping on the couch. It was a big one-bedroom apartment on the edge of Koreatown. It was entirely furnished with things from the Glendale townhouse, but they all looked different there. The couch we financed was there but darker than I remembered. Dirty. He didn't know to clean the couch cushions monthly. Our leaning bedroom floor mirror was hung in the living room, to refract light from his patio and brighten up the space. Our marital bed was now his alone, and next to it was our son's in its own little corner of the bedroom. Some things had been remodeled: The kitchen. The lighting. The bathroom hadn't been, and our son was not happy about it. All of his remembrance he had his own stone bathroom and jacuzzi tubs. When I moved out, he showered in my room in a standing shower—once freaking out because the linoleum chipped. Now at my new condo, we lived in a loft. His room was enormous with a brand-new, modern bathroom and his own spa shower. Here the shower was probably twenty-five years old. Rusted and peeling. He cried every time he had to bathe there. To make it easier on everyone, my ex would bathe him at my house at night and then take him home. I could tell it ate him up.

His new bachelor pad, with the faint smell of stale smoke from a previous tenant, felt safe. And homey. That's all that mattered to me. Our kid would not be jostled much more than he had already been. My ex figured that he would take the next few months to recoup from the move, then slowly try to get back on his feet. That was mid-February.

The virus changed everything. I knew there was no way that he was prepared to weather a month of no work. We couldn't have imagined how long it would be. I also knew the burden it would put on him to have to find ways to feed and care for our son in that time. He had driven Uber in the past when things were tight for us but had stopped shortly after we were married because his career was rolling. Since the separation, he had started again. Should he go back to make ends meet since there was no live music for the foreseeable future, he would be exposed every day and we could not let him see our son who had severe asthma. If he went home to his parents in Kansas City, I would be quarantined for who knew how long alone with our four-year-old while still working full time. The situation felt desperate. And again we sacrificed for each other. We made the decision to quarantine together.

He slept on the trundle of our son's bed for four months. My loft became a bed and breakfast. Everyone eating and sharing a common space together but retreating to their own rooms at night. We rarely fought and when we did it was calm and reminiscent of marital fights: him not doing the things he said he would re: putting away the dishes or cleaning. Discipline for our kid. Laziness. He would go home to get clothes. We used his fridge to store what mine couldn't hold. We never once slipped back into anything romantic. One night, I sat next to them while he was reading a book to our son in bed. His hand grazed my knee and I jumped, repulsed. We both felt the moment. I don't know if he intended to do it or if it was by accident. Either way he learned how I felt, if he hadn't known before. I couldn't see him like that anymore. We may have been back in roles we once had, but we were no longer who we once were.

There was nothing good about the death and fear that hammered away at the city that summer. We watched Italy, then New York bury their dead. Slowly those numbers made their way West. A few months later the racial unrest rocked us again, and we were beside ourselves. Still, something good was happening in my home. We had grown tremendously not being together anymore. He felt more chaotic to me now. That running and jumping into the ropes didn't feel courageous, it felt like folly. It seemed impulsive. I felt too particular to him. I overthought running and jumping. I was too meticulous to have any real fun. We had talked so much during our separation about how we felt that there was an ease now to calling each other's problem areas out. Each of us more accepting of the probability that we were doing "that thing we do that the other one hates." While we both wished for the pandemic to be over, it was nice to feel that feeling of home again, where someone is always there. There's always someone to sit with. We were careful to not cross boundaries of emotionally unloading with each other about too many personal things but knowing someone was there to do it with was wonderful to have again. We figured that was one of the reasons so many people stayed married so long. In the pandemic, watching people flounder out of aloneness shown a spotlight on how much love and intimacy we need to get by. And how little we actually know about how to do it without relationships. Even with them.

By June it became obvious that Safer at Home was going to be our way of life for quite a while. Unless we planned on making this a permanent situation, we had to devise a new plan where he could still help with childcare, I could still help with food and things, but he returned to his house. We worked it out quickly. Back to our regular custody schedule, but dinner at my house every day and on the days I worked, he would watch our son with me. I noticed a glimmer of sadness on his face when we settled it. I almost didn't ask if he was okay. Those questions always skirted the line of too much emotion. I asked.

He said, "I was driving home from my studio last week and I said to myself 'I hope we have food at home,' Then I realized I was referring to your house as home again. I knew this was coming. I was putting off the conversation."

I didn't clarify much. I assumed I understood. In our divorce we witnessed the miracle of marriage. How marriage should be. Had we known how to do it well when it was ours, it would have been really nice.

* * *

To have a Black family is to be royalty for us. If you have a home with a partner, a child, a dog, family photos that hang on the wall, and Saturday family plans you are a protected class. #CoupleGoals. #BlackLove. Entire shows are dedicated to highlighting well known couples and their "journeys" in staying together. We hear about the fighting. The infidelity. The moments of almost ending but sticking through it. Think pieces are written daily about how real love isn't perfect and the idea of a fairy tale will ruin your relationship.

I rarely see those think pieces circulating amongst my white friends.

White friends are still relatively new for me. Those closest to me are still in amazement that I have so many. In a television writer's room, we are divulging some of our deepest secrets and feelings for authentic storytelling. You grow close fast. It also results in an uncanny deep dive into the territory of white marriage and family. I've learned a lot.

White guys cry a lot. That trait I saw in my teenage years is not a pubescent quality that white men outgrow as they mature, it is a way of life. Their wives don't think they cry often—I mostly hear them say that they find them to be repressed. As a Black woman, I stress to my friends that they do. An awful lot. It's strange. Even the ones who don't cry that much have cried more in the last five years than most Black men will cry in their lifetime. The white men who never cry are probably pretty close with at least a couple Black men, even if it's only through a sports team.

I've also learned white women are *really* bossy. Not the way that turns young women into the next AOC, or the way that makes otherwise well-intentioned folks call a Black woman "intimidating" when she refuses to let someone play her, but the type of bossy that easily treads on you. The type that moves the toaster an inch to the right because it wasn't placed precisely where they wanted or who loudly proclaims to their friends that she *didn't* move the toaster because she "has to let him do things the way he does them." Neither seems to be ruining white marriages the way I was taught they would most assuredly ruin Black ones. I felt woefully misinformed.

Jumping in the ropes not only afforded me a window into white marriages, but also white motherhood. I belong to two distinctly different mommy groups online: one that is specifically for Black mothers and one that is not-so-specifically for white moms but most all are white. The differences are fascinating, specifically on topics of marriage. The Black women rarely bring up spouses or partners and when they do it is tempered. The praise for their partner abounds. The carefully crafted posts about what a "small issue" might be reeks of inauthenticity and I would find myself cringing before I would even read the comments or responses. Many would be about self-reflection—what more could she be doing. Lots of "better communication" or "prayer." And there would almost undoubtedly come a moment when someone may pepper the slightest bit of concern or "real talk" into a response and quickly be met with defensiveness.

"He's soooo good. We have so much fun together. He's such a good dad. He's living his dream. I don't want it to seem like I'm not happy, I would just feel a lot better if he didn't go on a week-long boys trip every month. He totally deserves it. I would never stop him. I just think maybe one of those months we could go somewhere. We go a lot of places. Lots of dates. Vacays. I don't know. I just . . . "

The scarier part to me would always be the women who would back her up, quietly reassuring her that no criticism of her husband would be tolerated and she didn't need to protect him in this "safe space." Over in the white mommy groups, women detailed how sex was stale. How they were scheduling sex to have it at all. How their hormone levels had dropped since the baby and they weren't in the mood anymore. Their partners wanted to have sex and they were having to discuss ways he could help her feel like doing it. Because it was the Sahara down there and if he couldn't help her do this, the drought would be worse for him than her. I texted my girl-friend Jennifer once. She was in both groups with me and I told her how wild I found the differences in our groups. I will never forget her response: "I aspire to be that free."

The white women I know have a freedom in life, and as a result love, that I have never had. They have the luck of being "desired" for their humanity. For their person. What makes a white woman desirable is not what she can do or bring or provide for the man in her life. It's her. Her personality. Her heart. Maybe her looks. How much fun she can be. Her outlook. Her likes and dislikes. Most don't have to "prove" they can be anything. They are not in competition with several other white women for some-one's affection. Love is not transactional but reciprocal. And should it not be reciprocated, they will leave, with the full knowl-edge that someone else can and will love them. They don't have to worry if their children will ever see a solid marriage or "white love." They are bombarded with it. They can be whoever they want to be, life's greatest prize, and anyone they can share that with is a sweet reminder of what life is all about.

We weren't taught that. Even if it was said to us it was not what was shown. When I first had my son, an aunt asked me how sex was post-child. I told her we weren't having sex yet. The doctor asked me to wait eight weeks. She looked at me in shock.

"I ain't never heard a Black man wait that long. Three weeks tops."

I asked a close male friend if he thought the same. He laughed and kind of shrugged it off. "If she's willing to do it, I have needs."

A year or so later, we were writing a scene for a show I wrote on and the topic came up. The retelling of that story made the white men in my writer's room—all fathers—nearly end the day. One cried. The room turned into an almost intervention, wondering if I had been abused. Because *that* was abusive to them. A woman was not yet healed after a major medical phenomenon. Sex too early could expose her to infection, improper healing, and pain. How could a man not control himself long enough to even chance that?! One man told me quietly later in my office that listening to me made him want to have the conversation with his newly married daughter.

I remember driving home that evening and trying to decide what I believed. On paper, I sided with the white people in my room. But it felt so weak. It felt weak to not bear that. It felt unsafe to allow your man to walk around with desires you couldn't fill—what if someone else did? It felt like "white people shit" for a husband to quietly let his bossy wife tell him when and where he would have a sexual urge. I considered my colleague, talking to his daughter about all of this. And how he was probably making Black people out to be monsters and I wished I never shared the story.

That was when it clicked. I wished I had not shared because the truth—our truth—was incorrect. What I had been taught was wrong. It was based on a misogynoir that was so part of my DNA that to attack it felt like you were attacking me and the people I loved. I felt defensive because had it not been for all that our ancestors had endured maybe this would have never happened. Maybe we wouldn't have had this thing wrong. How dare they be accusatory of us for behavior they created. Still, I wouldn't have that conversation with my daughter. I could never look my child in the eye and tell her, "Allow your husband to penetrate you before you're healed. He might leave otherwise." I would never. I would consider her husband unworthy of her if she had borne him a child—ravaged her body for their legacy—and he still deemed his carnal urges more important than her protection. What would he do if she had cancer? Was deployed or working far? Depressed? If her physical health was of no consequence to him, then he could never love her fully mentally or emotionally. He was consuming her. The conundrum of that moment made my heart race. I drove, raw, on a freeway, barely able to remember how I got home when I pulled into the driveaway. How could I learn a new thing if I defended the old? How could I not protect the old when it was a victim of abuse itself?

I knew some women who swore that they wanted to do it before the eight weeks. I'm sure it is possible. But sitting amongst free white women made it harder and harder for me to believe. They spoke so freely about sex. Some wanted to want to because sex was so "amazing" before children. Some would have the desire but the pain or anxiety of what might come after was too much. A sparse few did and were okay but would not in good conscience suggest it. Their marriages were not tethered to sex like ours were. Sex was wildly important. But it was not the anchor because most of their marriages were not a transaction. I had never known that kind of love. I doubted most of the women I knew did either.

For me, and for many of my contemporaries, we weren't quite willing to go as far as our mothers and grandmothers had gone. We wouldn't necessarily stay with a man who was a chronic adulterer or raging alcoholic or had some major deficiency that left our lives miserable. There was an awakening of our own power and worth. But we still held the image of the Black family in the highest regard. And we still had so few examples of healthy Black relationships that we were making up what we thought healthy to be. Standing by your husband through infidelity was considered "a thing that happens," and it most certainly is, but not nearly as often as we have to, nor to the degree. You would be hard pressed to find a Black woman who has not had some version of that issue with her husband. That very sentence sends white women into shock. The common response is, "Don't get it twisted. White people cheat, too." And they do. But it is not expected and far less tolerated.

Or maybe it is. I'm not white.

Still, we grit and bear that, or husbands who place their careers over family. We are so proud that they are men with aspirations we will bear their absenteeism. Or men who do not meet our love needs. We will remind ourselves that they are good to us and love us in their own way. We will detail all they've been through—how much better they are than their own fathers—and suppress their shortcomings in ways they would never allow us to fall short. Of course, these things aren't uniquely Black. They happen in every race. But the frequency with which I see Black women—my sisters—deal is beyond anecdotal and can never be qualified because, like the mommy group comments, we struggle to go on record about it. To call it what it is feels like betrayal. So we won't. We'd rather not call it anything than to shake the foundation of our family. Of the miracle.

We are trying to be the Black elite. We want to be the exception to the rule. The family that stayed together. The #CoupleGoals. The #BlackLove. Our hearts are our living sacrifice for the picture we can give our children of marriage. One that's not perfect but real. We've yet to realize that by glorifying the length of time we stayed married over the healthiness of the marriage is creating the worst foundation for our children yet. As we fight for their freedom in the world at large, we are shackling their spirits, their hearts, and their emotions. If we are successful at finding them physical freedom—the ability to walk freely throughout the country and rise to anything they want or to simply be—but have failed to show them how to properly love and respect one another's boundaries and expectations and commitments, then what have we done? When a young Black man or Black woman is allowed to feel hurt, anger, pain, joy, and happiness and own it, to demand their person be loved correctly and have that demand met with respect, that's freedom. That might be why marriage—in the way that we have come to know it—has become less attractive to so many. Generations yell at us that we lack commitment or the ability to sacrifice. Some of that may be true. But wanting a love that does not require hushed conversations in bedrooms or think pieces and documentaries to understand does not seem like an unreasonable ask. It seems like freedom. Perhaps the picture we've created of Black love has turned into our bondage.

* * *

I DID NOT LEAVE MY COUCH for a week when I decided to file for divorce. It felt as though the blood had been sucked from my veins and there was a deflated, lackluster version of me unable to move until someone pumped life back into it. I wasn't heartbroken anymore. I was never actually presently conscious of any heartbreak throughout the entire ordeal. I would always notice the heartbreak after. A week. A month. I would be explaining to someone an argument we had or an event that took place and in describing my personal feelings would have no word other than "heartbroken."

I waited six months before filing. In the beginning I could not admit to myself that I was hoping we could stay married. By the time of filing I could say it. There wasn't much to work out. The depth of the betrayal and the length of the dishonesty was too much to apologize for. What I believed to be the saving grace was that none of my ex's transgressions came from a place of malice or irreverence. He was a man who was deeply wounded, lost, and trying to present as more confident and adult-like than he had ever felt comfortable being. His awkwardness and his being "just left of center" were what people loved about him most. It was endearing to watch someone meander almost innocently through life. All of that was real and true. What was also true was that it was not a personality trait the way we all had seen. The way I saw it for many years. It was his true self. He didn't have childlike enthusiasm. It was the enthusiasm of a child. Someone who had yet to go past a certain level of his own life because of things he had yet to share with anyone. Things he could barely say to himself. I obviously understood that.

So I waited. Not for us to work out. There was no way that could happen. But to meet who he really was. Who was the grown-up version of the man I had spent the last decade with? What did the mature version look like? What did a healed him have to offer? Would we even still like each other? For the sake of our miracle and that of my sons, I thought I owed him some time to find out. For my own healing, I could not allow myself to move a moment faster than I was ready to.

What I remember most about that time is the extremity with which people wanted me to move. There were of course those that wanted me to divorce immediately. Cut ties and losses, take the kid and jet. They weren't wrong in their advice. I was well within my rights to do that. The shock of his other life was so deep, I often worried that he had the capacity to make sound decisions at all and what that meant for our child. But it was the wrong answer. One of my closest friends relayed a story to me in that time. The officiant of her wedding was a close friend whose wife had a brazen affair. When he caught her, she admitted to it and was adamant that she would continue. Like the stencil on the wall of my friend's mother room, the husband never gave up, even when the wife did. They never gave up on the same day. The couple reconciled. My friend purposely chose them as "mentors" for her marriage because of their ability to love each other through their worst. That story was awe-inspiring to her. Of course people worked through affairs all the time, but she knew about this one. My friend is white. I didn't have the heart to tell her how many stories I had like that, with one glaring difference: the one who cheated was always the man. But I held on to that story nevertheless.

I was simultaneously put off by the people who thought it best that we stay together. As if the betrayals had not happened. Who tried to headshake his bad behavior away. Who placed the image of our "Black family" over my humanity and my heart, or who swore to me that one day my heart would heal and, "Wouldn't I be so glad to still have him? This family?" I never understood that, either. I was broken. I questioned how much someone could really love me to watch my ex blow us to smithereens and then ask me to collect the bloodied pieces of carnage, stitch myself back together, then use my unsealed fingers to do the same for him. I was convinced that those people didn't love me. Even if I chose to stay, I would have still believed that. They loved the idea of us—the look, the Black family—so much that they would allow us to die, smiling in frame, before getting out of this thing alive but with the "shame" of having not lasted. Some even asked us to "separate in home" so people wouldn't know. We could hide that.

Even in writing this I feel my blood boil. My brow is furrowed and the keys pound. They never cared how we fared as people. How our hearts were. How we came out on the other side. Whatever needed to happen, whoever needed to lie to themselves to keep our Black family intact would have to bite the bullet. *That* was more important than our persons. I had done that throughout my marriage. I knew what it was like to be so close to emotional and spiritual death that there was no way it would be me. I needed the space to heal not just from the lies but from the years. He did not know how to sacrifice. The Black love he had been taught never called for that. It couldn't be him. We were at an impasse and it didn't feel like anyone was helping us.

It didn't matter anyway.

He didn't heal. At least not then. Trauma is tricky. It can send you headfirst into a therapist's chair or running for the hills to avoid all the terrible feelings it stirs up. It made him do the latter. He wasn't horrible or less apologetic or mean. At first, he would ask everyday if we could try again. Then it stopped. He tells me now that, at that time, hearing that he must first act before he could get what he wanted felt like rejection. He was so used to being able to "promise" better without having to *be* better that it seemed anyone requiring the action must already know he would not deliver. So you were essentially telling him no. I once asked if it ever dawned on him that he was the issue. That he was not hearing "no," but was in fact hearing a tentative "yes" contingent upon his doing what he said he would do. He looked at me. He thought for a moment.

"No. I never thought of it like that."

Those were our impossible odds. I wasn't fighting against infidelity or domestic imbalances. I was fighting against the deep-seated belief that all he had to do was show up. I was fighting against years and decades and a century of women choking back their own lives and hearts and futures to simply be in the presence of a "husband." To have a "Black family." But I was not those women. The hammer finally fell on the weekend of the Emmy Awards. I had been nominated the year before. He took a show out of state and left me with our son to sort it all out myself that weekend. His mother offered to buy him a ticket so he could escort me. He declined. After a couple of years of therapy, we got to the bottom of it: the attention being squarely on me had made him uncomfortable. It didn't show up in any overt way. He was always beaming, always proud. But it manifested quietly in his spirit. When I wasn't there to answer a call because I was in an interview, he would find someone to talk to. Of course that behavior already existed prior to my career growth. When I couldn't answer because I was bathing our son or had to be asleep earlier because he woke up at six in the morning, he would find someone. When I would ask him to take part in the things at home as best he could from the road and he thought me asking too much, he would find someone. When he felt generally overwhelmed, as he often did, and I didn't assuage his reluctance to responsibility, he would find someone.

We taught men this. Like the day I drove home, trying to remove the sticky tack of the bad behavior of sex before healing and white people calling out that behavior, I was stuck again. When one thought released itself from my hand, it would affix itself to the other. The next finger. And I'd be fastened in a new way. A different way. It was impossible. There was no way for my ex to know how to love outside of transaction because he had never seen it. He had only known how to find ways to meet his needs, to swallow back his emotions, and to present as well as humanly possible. The only way to overcome that was to break it. To break it meant to break us. Which squarely placed us in the middle of what our folks deemed "failure." The thing that makes transactional love be withheld. Impossible. Impossible.

When I was nominated for a second Emmy, we were separated. He stayed in town this time, feeble attempts to prove he could be supportive. He was there when I got home. I would not let him escort me. He lost that privilege. I noticed his mood was different than everyone else who was there to greet me. He seemed happy but despondent. At some point we discussed it. He sadly admitted he was struggling with my winning the Emmy. He felt I had not emphasized him enough throughout the win. I had not thanked him at the after party. Hadn't thanked him for keeping our child when I worked. I grew irate. I asked him to point to—specifically—what he had done to deserve any acknowledgment. I hadn't lived with him in over six months and had slept in a different room for two months prior. The four months before that, when I filmed the show I was awarded for, he was on tour. I had no clue what part of that he could be asking for me to proclaim. He wasn't even upset at my line of questioning. My voice shook as I demanded his answer. We were in the old townhouse then. I was dressed for an interview. He looked at the black granite, the same one his watch laid on that day the message notification went off.

Without looking up he said, "I didn't do anything. I keep having to have quick calls with my therapist because I'm trying to figure out how I know all of that and still feel like you owe me something. I'm having to stop myself from wanting attention elsewhere."

I admired his honesty but hated his truth. It was growth. And that growth showed me we couldn't stay married. I filed for divorce that Monday.

When I laid on my couch, lamenting my marriage, I knew I wouldn't miss any of that. There was nothing to miss. I didn't feel heartbroken. I didn't miss him. Instead, I mourned everything that could have been. What we were on the brink of. What may have transpired had he done the work. Or never done the dirt. What could we have been? Who could he have been? What was next? All I knew is that I chose me. I knew that to many people that meant I failed. That our Black family failed. That we had not been able to persevere somehow. But that wasn't true. This was our first taste of freedom. This was our first shot at breaking the bonds of "presenting Black family" and learning how to love correctly. It had to start with a breaking. So I broke on my couch.

* * *

A Letter to Everyone Who Has Advised Me on Love:
Below, please find a passage from Bible:

Proverbs 31
The Sayings of King Lemuel

1   The sayings of King Lemuel contain this message,
    which his mother taught him.

2   O my son, O son of my womb,
    O son of my vows,

3   do not waste your strength on women,
    on those who ruin kings.

4   It is not for kings, O Lemuel, to guzzle wine.
    Rulers should not crave alcohol.

5   For if they drink, they may forget the law
    and not give justice to the oppressed.

6   Alcohol is for the dying,
    and wine for those in bitter distress.

7   Let them drink to forget their poverty
    and remember their troubles no more.

8   Speak up for those who cannot speak for
        themselves;
    ensure justice for those being crushed.

9   Yes, speak up for the poor and helpless,
    and see that they get justice.

A Wife of Noble Character

10 Who can find a virtuous and capable wife?
    She is more precious than rubies.

11 Her husband can trust her,
    and she will greatly enrich his life.

12 She brings him good, not harm,
    all the days of her life.

13 She finds wool and flax
    and busily spins it.

14 She is like a merchant's ship,
    bringing her food from afar.

15 She gets up before dawn to prepare breakfast
        for her household
    and plan the day's work for her servant girls.

16 She goes to inspect a field and buys it;
    with her earnings she plants a vineyard.

17   She is energetic and strong,
      a hard worker.

18   She makes sure her dealings are profitable;
      her lamp burns late into the night.

19   Her hands are busy spinning thread,
      her fingers twisting fiber.

20   She extends a helping hand to the poor
      and opens her arms to the needy.

21   She has no fear of winter for her household,
      for everyone has warm clothes.

22   She makes her own bedspreads.
      She dresses in fine linen and purple gowns.

23   Her husband is well known at the city gates,
      where he sits with the other civic leaders.

24   She makes belted linen garments
      and sashes to sell to the merchants.

25   She is clothed with strength and dignity,
      and she laughs without fear of the future.

26   When she speaks, her words are wise,
      and she gives instructions with kindness.

27   She carefully watches everything in her
          household
      and suffers nothing from laziness.

28   Her children stand and bless her.
      Her husband praises her:

29   "There are many virtuous and capable women
          in the world,
      but you surpass them all!"

30 Charm is deceptive, and beauty does not last;
   but a woman who fears the Lord will be greatly
      praised.

31 Reward her for all she has done.
   Let her deeds publicly declare her praises.

You taught me, at times berated me with the idea, that I was to model myself after the Proverbs 31 woman. That is who I should be, and the attributes outlined in the biblical verses should be whom every man should be looking to make his wife. Upon reading for myself with a now critical eye, I have several questions. These questions are enumerated below:

1. When the wife is doing all the spinning and selling, who is watching her children?

2. When the wife is planning the day for her "servants," who is paying them for their time?

3. Does her husband feel like he's paying too much? Or is that coming out of her earnings?

4. If her candle doesn't go out at night doing all that spinning, is her husband peeved (peeved-eth?) that she isn't readily available for his sexual needs while she's trying to sew the comforter? Or does she stop, do that, then go back to sewing?

5. When does she sleep?

6. Is her husband sitting with the elders all day? While she's doing all this running around? Oh no . . . he's working as well. Strike five from the questions.

6. This field inspecting and purchasing vineyards and such . . . does she have to discuss this with her husband before she does it?

If Yes: That means he has to be home at some point. And engaging with her daily. Listening to the stories of her day and truly caring about what she's doing. Cool. Sounds cool.

If No: Well that's fine. He may be sitting with the Elders too much and he's cool with her doing whatever.

Apart from the questions dealing directly with the "wife" portion of the scripture, I ask that you enlighten me on the first ten verses. From my understanding, the Proverb is written by a king, retelling the advice his mother gave him.

She begins by saying, "Look Lem, stop chasing women and trying to validate yourself through sexual pleasure. These women you're running with want to keep you out all night drinking and dancing. That is not the type of stuff kings do. That stuff is for the lower class. The people that need your help as a leader, they need to drink and party because they are trying to forget their problems. Your job is to solve their problems."

That's it right? That is what she's saying? Then she outlines for him the type of woman that he "should" be looking for. One that we must assume is vastly different than the women he has been keeping company with. A woman who will be working equally as hard as him if he were doing what it is that he ought to.

Now I ask you, in light of all of this, why is Proverbs 31 preached at women's conferences? And taught to little girls? And framed in rose gold metallics over toilets and stitched into throw blankets sold for Mother's Day? Why is this not at the men's retreats? Why does every Black boy that grew up in church have the ability to recite, "Charm is deceptive and beauty is fleeting," but has no clue that only twenty verses earlier, in the same chapter, the thought that led to the thought, was that certain actions were unbecoming of him. It seems that the chapter was written for men, not women. Written to recognize that the life they want, the prestige they want, the family they want is on the other side of them learning their purpose in the world—their importance in the world—and committing to both that and one woman. Together they will take care of each other, their family, and their work. King Lemuel's mother is abundantly clear: these women already exist. Her son is just not picking them. Or maybe he's mistreating them. I dare not wade into hearsay but it seems likely.

How did this become about us? How did Proverbs 31 become the clarion call for women to maintain a perfect image of self, marriage, and household? It's clear as day in the text. This is about men being better.

Specifically Black men. Because everyone in the Bible is Black. I'll discuss in my next letter.

—*Vanessa*

* * *

Tonight, I am painfully lonely.

I laid in bed after my ex left and realized this would have been the month of my anniversary. I had no clue when it was. Either August 24th or the 26th. It was far too long ago to check any social media, so I checked my divorce decree. I had a PDF copy on my phone for business I had to handle separating our assets.

I wanted my ex to stay tonight. Not because I love him. Or even like him that much. But because even in our silence and being on opposite ends of the house, there is a familiarity in his presence. Having to create a life separate from him was not the hardest job of divorce. It was having to acknowledge that every dream and desire may now be altered. Some could happen as planned. Others would look different. Some reimagined entirely. We had just bought a fridge. It felt like our first adult purchase. Not financed. Not budgeted. We got the fridge we wanted. Two swinging doors. Ice maker and water tap. Drawer freezer. For both of us, those fridges were the sign of wealth when we were kids. It oddly felt like we made it. When we moved out of our town-house, both of us found apartments that had fridges inside. Two months after purchase, I left that fridge. A year later he sold it. What felt like the beginning of everything we had ever dreamed about, beginning with Whirlpool appliances, slid back into pre-parenthood. We had owned every fridge we had since we were married. But here we were again. When would I be in a position to brazenly buy something like that again? Would I do it in another apartment? A house? Would I have another partner? Another child? Would I even live in Los Angeles? All the things I had figured out before, I didn't know.

When he was at my house through the pandemic, it seemed rude to say those thoughts out loud. The divorce was still fresh enough that we should be considerate of one another's healing. Four months together meant I didn't have to discuss any of my concerns for a post-marriage life out loud. They went essentially unthought about as well. I had the chance to slip back into a pseudo-marriage state. There was no physical touch, but there were two parents in the home. My ex had a safe place to land but could mentally check out without being bothered. We were back to our old Black love. Experiencing the miracle again.

The loneliness was also the same. The gnawing of sitting in your own home with another adult and being unable to connect in any meaningful way. When we were together, I would try and find ways. Cooking things he liked. Planning outings. Trips. Watching movies. Anything to engage him. It felt like part of the job. I was told it was part of the job. "Find ways to keep it spicy. Do things to remind him you are still fun." I never did the things that engaged my heart and my mind. He would not have joined me. He didn't know those things and would never venture far from what he knew. He only kept friends like that too. Friends that would dip a toe in intimate friendships but whose fear of the unknown kept them scoffing at anything that resembled an unveiling of something they needed to unlearn. Friends on the sidelines. I would cater to them as well, hoping that deeper friendships and people he could open up to would somehow solve the problem of his aloofness. An aloofness he had also learned. We had both learned so many things that needed to be unlearned. I set myself on fire to keep him warm for a decade because that is what I was taught.

I was not able to do that again. I found so many lost pieces. They had been gone so long I was trying to get reacquainted. I could not risk losing them again. He had to. He was learning, albeit slowly, that his need for comfort was failing him. But he was in the midst of the lesson. I was beyond that. I had packed my things and started again. There was no way familiarity would send me scattered again. No matter how lonely I could get without another adult human, it would never match the kind of lonely I felt when my presence was not enough. When my best was never enough. When no matter how much of a Proverbs 31 woman I was or how perfectly I presented "Black love" it was not enough, but I was still expected to present it. Because my life was not worth enough. My life had to be sacrificed for the "whole." A whole that was broken and pillaged since its arrival on colonial shores. Everyone carried on and called it "normal" and "the way things are," but now I had tasted how things could be. Even in divorce I saw a healthier love and knew it possible. There is no worse lonesomeness than when you have abandoned yourself and no one even notices you are missing. But here I was. If no one else ever realized I was absent from my own life again, I surely wouldn't be that person. Not even for Black love. Because I am Black. And loving my Black-ass self has proven equally as revolutionary as being able to maintain the miracle of Black marriage. Perhaps, it would even be the answer to how to maintain that miracle. To love me so much that for someone to have access to all of me they would have to love me as much as I did. So I chose lonely. I choose lonely.

That is why I let him go tonight. That is why my hands gripped the kitchen island as my son's snoring hummed throughout my house. That is why I quietly climbed into bed tonight, then got up again and carried my giant child into my own bed. To feel close to something and someone. To remind myself that someone cares that I am here for more reasons than what I can provide. That I am home to someone, too.

Tonight I looked at my divorce papers. We were married on the 24th.

Next week.

Tomorrow I will ask him if he forgets the date too.

SIX

JOGGERS

The emergence of white girls jogging down Crenshaw was the first sign of trouble.

We had lived in Hyde Park, an area of South Los Angeles that bordered Inglewood, for about two years at that time. I was pregnant. We had every intention of staying in the area, raising our son there, and planting roots. But those damn joggers.

I remember the first time we saw one. Her white earbuds visible as the strawberry blonde ponytail swayed with every counted step, blissfully unaware of the number of Black and brown faces watching her from their driveways or windows or porches. Maybe she wasn't blissfully unaware. Maybe she was hyper-aware, the headphones a purposeful distraction from what she felt were unwelcoming faces. Perhaps she feared what we all were thinking. Her running in the Crenshaw District would be considered dangerous to anyone who knew her, but maybe she was determined to not let fear of the unknown and preconceived notions of "neighborhoods like this" deter her. And good for her if that were the case. Of course, we are not allowed that same privilege. Our running or jogging, lost in the music of our phones or even our own thoughts, can be a death sentence for us, as was the case with Ahmaud Arbery. At minimum it would mean that someone may call the police—a suspicious face in the neighborhood—and we have to somehow prove that despite the fears of concerned citizens we are not violating any laws. For this young woman, if she had been frightened (which I'll never know), her fear was of us.

To be clear, we were scared of her, too.

I stood at my car, pregnant, preparing to go to work. At the time, my ex-husband RJ and I shared a car. A young married couple cutting their teeth in Hollywood, a baby on the way, we had a mint green Prius with 75,000 miles on it. Miles accrued from driving Uber and delivering cupcakes for a local errand company to make ends meet. From shoots around the city. Gigs even further. But we did it, and we were making it, and our entire community was proud of us. With the baby on the way, we had just started considering a second car. There were two in-home daycares on our block. Our son would go to one for a while. The neighbors down the street kept bringing us baby stuff. The neighbor across from us convinced me daily to "walk that baby down." I'd waddle up and down our block every night. A few would come to their porches as I slowly made my way and would ask how I was doing, offering remedies for swollen feet or to induce labor. The neighbor caddy-corner to us, Keisha, is who suggested it was time for a second vehicle.

"If you're at work and she's home who gets the car? She may need you to pick something up for the baby on the way home. Or what if there's an emergency and she needs to leave?" A few months later we got a small SUV.

But this day we stood at the Prius and watched this woman jog bye. We turned to our neighbors two houses east. They were outside too. That neighbor worked full time but was a musician in another life. When we first moved in, we turned a room in our house into a studio for RJ. One night, he was loudly playing drums, recording a song for an artist he was working with, and we never considered that the noise may be bleeding outside. When there was a knock on the door, that concept crystalized. We readied ourselves for whatever we might hear. It was that neighbor, a brother in his late thirties or early forties, with wine in hand.

"We hear you down the street."

"Sorry about that," RJ replied.

"No, no man, you sound great. All of us are listening. Wanted to bring this over and welcome you to the neighborhood. I play sax. Maybe we can get together and jam sometimes."

They never actually got together. But when RJ would play, you could wait, and a few moments later you'd hear the faint sound of a saxophone. If you stepped onto the street from your own porch, you could see a few people sitting outside, enjoying the concert. By the second week of being in the neighborhood, everyone would ask, "You the boy that bangs on them drums? You sound good. Who you play for?" A few months in and everyone knew us and always looked out. When work picked up and RJ was on tour, folks would tell me they missed him playing. It was the saxophonist that we first caught eyes with when the jogger passed. He just laughed and shook his head. RJ did the same.

If this woman was a new resident of Hyde Park, their neighborhood jam session days were numbered.

Of course, they could still do it. But there was a good chance that the police would be called for noise pollution. No one in our neighborhood wanted police presence. Ever. To pretend that our block, or the surrounding blocks were some middle-America Mayberry with white picket fences and unlocked doors would be a gross exaggeration and frankly a mischaracterization. We had our troubles. The unsavory. The folks you wished would stop cutting up (a Black colloquialism that I refuse to explain). There were people we knew to not engage. A house, left to the family of the owner long deceased, that would be frequently occupied by her grandson and his friends. He was banging (re: Black colloquialism). But the men (and a few women) on the block, talked to him regularly. "Pick up the trash." "You can't speed down the street, there are babies playing here." "Be respectful of the neighborhood." He rarely listened but he never scoffed. He had a friend with him once, a young woman. She was probably nineteen. I don't know where she was from, but she didn't understand the rules of our neighborhood. She double parked and Keisha told her she was blocking a homeowner in. The young girl mouthed off and Keisha proceeded to whoop her ass. I mean, it wasn't even fair. I distinctly remember Keisha losing her shirt in the fight. Her breast flailed with every punch and eventually she sent the woman inside crying. We all watched from our houses. Somehow Keisha's shirt disappeared and she stood there in the middle of the street, hands on her hips, bare chested and winded. I don't know who it was that yelled, "Keisha, put some clothes on," but the whole block laughed. The grandson apologized for what happened a few days later. We bought Keisha a bottle of vodka for her trouble.

No one double-parked again.

We handled our block in-house. Our neighbors were our job. It would have been nice to have some higher authority who could help sometimes, but that was not safe for us. The notoriety of the corrupt LAPD is more than hyperbole, it is fact. Should our neighbors have not liked the drumming from our home, we would have heard about it. But no one would have dared called the police. The loitering. The double-parking. Never. We would handle that. While I will not speak for other blocks or neighborhoods in South LA, I can say that, in 2015, our reluctance to call the authorities had nothing to do with a fear of retaliation of any gang violence.

It was the fear of white people coming into our neighborhood with any authority.

A year before the white girl started jogging, we were put on lockdown for an entire night. The story we heard was that an LAPD officer driving on Crenshaw and MLK had managed to dislodge his service rifle from his police motorcycle. It dropped somewhere in the intersection. By the time he noticed and came back, it was gone (of course). They locked South LA down. We were not allowed to come in or out of our homes as they searched for their missing gun. There were choppers all night. Police dogs. RJ's best friend Arty was at our house using his drums. He didn't live in South LA, and the constant bullhorns and lights from the helicopters trying to save LAPD from a lawsuit made him uneasy. He decided to go home and come back some other time. When RJ went to walk him out, they were surrounded by police, German Shepherds snarling.

"Get your asses back in the house!"

"I'm just leaving."

"No one is coming in or out until we say so!"

"You can't tell me I can't go home. I don't live here. I haven't done anything wrong!"

"If you move, we will release the dogs!"

RJ dragged Arty back into the house before his mouth could make him a hashtag. He wasn't wrong. The entire situation was wrong. An officer made a mistake, so they unlawfully locked us down. Threatened attacks (not detainment) for not following orders. We were all angry but had no recourse. All we could do was wait them out and keep our heads down. They could do whatever they wanted here. You couldn't call *them* to help you treat the wound *they* inflicted. All you could do was hope that you would see them as little as possible and treat your wounds yourself.

The appearance of the white woman jogger meant they were coming. White people trust that authority—they have no reason not to—and feel that the recourse for a neighborhood disturbance is to call the police. Culturally, their idea of a neighborhood disturbance is different than our own. When I was eight months pregnant, the house behind ours had a party. My son was giant and pushed my hips out of place, making my spine to pelvis an "S" shape. I barely got any sleep due to the pain of carrying him. To have a party going all night only made what little sleep I could get impossible. But the DJ (there was a whole-ass DJ) kept repeating that it was someone's 50th birthday and they were going to party until the sun came up. They did. And I carried my giant ass to the couch and dozed off there. One more night of no sleep wasn't worth someone's mom/aunt/grandma/sister/whoever not being celebrated surviving until fifty. We threw parties like that for our family, too. We would have never wanted to be shut down. I'm assuming the rest of the neighborhood felt the same way because they didn't end until 5 a.m. While that might have disturbed some of us, it was not a "disturbance." Our privilege was not so unchecked that we felt as though enduring a few hours or a night of conditions not being exactly what we wanted was some kind of infringement on our rights. If my child didn't get to nap at exactly noon, or if I was a little tired for work the next day because of some happening in our neighborhood, that was fine every once in a while. Should a problem persist, I could go and tell my neighbor, a person I more than likely already had a relationship with.

The white jogger, in our summation, would not feel the same.

First, she would fear most of us. There would be very little "getting to know you." The move to Hyde Park was an economic one. Everyone was being priced out of the burgeoning "hipster" pockets and we were next on the docket. We had escaped gentrification for quite some time. South LA is *so* Black, even gentrifiers wondered if their coming would make it "safe enough." But then the Los Angeles Rams. The stadium. The bid for the Olympics. There was too much economic opportunity and they started coming regardless. West Adams. Then Jefferson Park. They moved further and further south. This was the farthest south I had ever seen a white person. I worked three miles away, in nearby Culver City. That's where the white people were. Houses there were at least double the price, but they would never cross Slauson Avenue. That would transport them to a different world. There did not exist a single person who would move to this neighborhood—renter or otherwise—who would not have known that coming in. Who would not have heard "do not move there." Who would not have heard the commentary about the civil unrest in 1991. Who would not have at the very least considered that before moving.

She feared us. Her bravery in living in Hyde Park resulted from her knowing that she had recourse with the police, who we feared above all. She was a threat.

Secondly, none of us knew her. Our first introduction to the white jogger was that jog. Her singular, focused jog. Culturally, we give a head nod when we see folks we don't know. From coast to coast a head nod to another Black man or woman is a customary greeting. On the street. At a stop light. In a store. It's an acknowledgment that we see each other, we are on the same page, and the same team. Sometimes it's subtle, barely visible if you don't know what you are looking for. Sometimes it's grand, a tiny bow of the neck, enthusiastically welcoming your presence. But it's there. For Black women, we sometimes don't nod to one another but catch eyes. I can't explain "the look," but every Black woman knows it. We say, "I see you, sis," with a flick of an iris. If the woman is older, we smile: a gesture of reverence, telling her we respect her. I may even ask how she is doing. A complete stranger, but in my mind an elder. An aunt. My now-four-year-old used to watch me in those situations and ask if we knew "that lady." I used to say no. That we are just being friendly. Now I say yes.

Beyond how we have to show up to create a safe space for each other, we all recognize the need to appear non-threatening to white people. I have a very specific smile and voice for white folks. RJ, who weighs 145 pounds on the best day and to Black people is perhaps the single least scary person on the planet, is overly polite. Regardless of how we see him, he is hyper aware that he is a brown-skinned Black man with dreadlocks, and that carries a stigma. I have a friend who is six-foot-four and practices meditation every day. He is a writer and knows that if he were ever defensive of his work he would be seen as angry, so he appears in the world zen, even if he isn't, for his own safety. Still I have other friends, who I admire greatly, that choose to not appear as anything but their natural Black selves. They are the pinnacle of personal success in my mind. I have often wished that I had their bravery. They know that appearing that way in the world carries the consequence of white fear and judgement. They don't care (nor should they have to). But they are still aware of it. They have no choice but to be. For a Black person to show up fully as themselves in the world is a risk and they would be foolish to not have counted the costs of that. Should they receive unfair treatment, they are armed with facts about biases being projected upon them. They are ready. Because they know.

The white jogger never had to consider that. Never did she feel the need to acknowledge us, to look to the left or to the right. She was focused on one goal and that was to run. What a privilege. She may have had legitimate concerns. The fear that someone would attack *her*. She lives in a world where she has come to believe that her personhood is a treasure. Something so valuable and precious that someone may try to take it from her without her permission. I certainly don't discredit that. I'm a woman. I know that fear. But as a *Black* woman, my fear differs. Should something like that happen to me, would anyone close notice that I was in trouble or would they believe me "strong enough to handle myself?" Would anyone here help me if they feared me? Was I even the right type of "pretty" for a rapist to want to attack me? I had to first consider my Blackness before my womanhood.

Her womanhood was her most precious commodity. She was the lily in the valley of her world. Worthy of protection. Should someone violate her, her children, her comfort, her right to do whatever-the-fuck, she would raise hell. March herself to that police station. If they wouldn't listen, she'd converge on the local news. If that wasn't enough, she would gather those like-minded and set the world on fire. She didn't *have* to know us. She didn't have to acknowledge us. She could pick and choose who she cared to speak to, when she cared to speak, what people she chose to get to know beyond stereotype, because no one could touch her. If they did, she had a plan.

We couldn't do that. We couldn't go tell a police officer we were harassed by a white person. The media would ignore us. We could link arms with our kinfolk, but unless some bleeding-heart white reporter decided to cover it, it would be "Black news." We would have to protest—block a street, take a knee— to get any mainstream coverage, and Colin Kaepernick showed us the consequences of that. Our protests somehow made us "ungrateful" for our rights. Rights we don't even fully have.

Whether that white jogger realized it or not, she didn't have to know us because she was armed. The world was in her favor. She was a threat.

Thirdly, and most importantly to us, her presence required a censorship of self. That censorship made our community less safe for us and more safe for her and people like her. To avoid the calls to police or the worry of them coming to our neighborhood, we would have to do things less like ourselves. Block parties and kids doing wheelies down the street might be winding down. But the thing that we dreaded, the part that at very least ate me up, was that protecting the young man banging across the street would be gone too. That might sound crazy to people who aren't Black. Most of us don't want those young men and women currently lost to the streets to go to jail any more than we want them living reckless. What we want is the ability to show them something different. To provide opportunities and resources for them to have other options. To give them examples of other ways. We can't do that if we can't touch them. We can't touch them if they are not in our neighborhoods. White neighbors make it unsafe for them to be *home*. A "simple call" to police to check on noise or too many cars could end in arrest or worse. A knock on the door by a vigilant white person asserting their "rights as home-owners" in our neighborhood might end in a fist fight like it did with Keisha. What we've learned from Trayvon and now Ahmaud Arbery is that a white person losing a fist fight to a Black man makes him fear for his life, a now justifiable means to kill a Black body. A white neighbor means censorship, or your life could be at stake. They are threats.

Most of these young men and women are not crazy. They are not without conscience or spirit or ability to reason. But their world view is not that of a white jogger, perpetually protected, who has the privilege of being concerned about their health. They are considering where they fit in a world that continuously bombards them with images and rhetoric of how unimportant and how useless their lives are unless they can somehow benefit white people. If they aren't attending a college or university, running a ball, or entertaining someone, what are they here for? They have seen more videos of them being killed in the street and the killers going free than they have of any white body fighting for their lives. Why would they go out of their way to make a white girl who can't say "hello" feel safe? She certainly has not done the same for them. But if they make the choice to *not* speak, to not bow to white supremacy, to take up space and make the same assertions that nationalists make about assimilation—"You moved to my neighborhood. Learn *this* language. Learn *this* place."—they are considered unwelcoming and scary and that makes them a walking, breathing, target. If we do not censor who we are and assimilate to who whites want us to be to feel safe, it is a green light for oppression. A green light for death.

A brave Black person is a threat. That white jogger symbolized death. Death of freedom or physical death. Our personal choices would determine which we'd experience.

When we got into the car that day, we drove silently for a few blocks.

RJ looked at me and said, "Is it time to start thinking of another place to live? Someplace safer?"

"It's this or places where white people run every day. This is the safest place."

"Yeah but that's a beast we know."

"Is it?"

We didn't talk about it much after that. A few more moved in. Inglewood began gentrifying. And by the time my son was three months old there was a raid on the house across the street. The grandson and a bunch of his friends, hands zip-tied behind their backs, sat on our lawn while the police did something inside. We don't know what. Keisha yelled to them to not say a word until they got lawyers. The block watched. Some recorded. But it was pretty clear none of us had called the police. I heard some weeks later that all of them were released but the damage was done, to their psyche and to our little utopia. RJ called me at work that day and told me we were moving. Not because the kids across the street made us feel unsafe, rather because he didn't want our son seeing images of Black men being treated that way in his own neighborhood. The world was going to tell him that. We had to protect his image of being Black in America for as long as we could. We moved three months later to a place where white joggers ran every day. Slews of them. A neighborhood where we were a threat, but we knew how to disarm with smiles and higher-pitch voices and Disney-level chipperness and charm. The beast we knew.

As I grieved Ahmaud Arbery, it became painfully clear that we did not know that beast at all. Performing whiteness doesn't save us. Staying in our own communities doesn't save us. Going to theirs is worse. If a white person decides that they want what we have, that they want to occupy the space we are in, if they simply don't approve of *how* we take up space, they can take it. If we fight for it—fight for our lives or our livelihood—we are a threat. Not capitulating to their desires is aggressive and aggression can be met with force. Supremacy is real. And like Black Wall Street, Rosewood—hell, Leimert Park—when they see opportunity in our fortune or simply feel as though we have forgotten our place, when two or three armed white men feel like a Black man running has to do what they say to assuage their fears or they are licensed to kill, we see supremacy at work. An unknown white woman jogging in a neighborhood of color was a warning shot.

The morning after the videotape of Ahmaud Arbery's death was released, I went for a jog in my now very white, affluent neighborhood in Los Angeles. I laced up my shoes and jogged until I couldn't. Then I walked. I wouldn't normally have done that alone. I fear for my safety as a Black person and as a woman. But I pushed past it. I walked past a vegan restaurant. A doggy daycare. Multi-million-dollar homes and a CBD oil boutique. I counted fourteen white joggers. I didn't move off of the sidewalk for any of them. I didn't say hello to them or anyone along the way. No smiles. No head nods. Nothing to make them feel that I was a "good Black," I honestly didn't care what the fuck they thought about me that day. I was hurting and I was being reckless. I wondered to myself more times than I would like to admit if I was being stupid. I had a child at home that needed his mother to come home alive. But rage drove me. The rage of seeing Ahmaud's crumpled body in the street. The rage of feeling like the neighborhood I loved the most was stripped from me. The rage of knowing that I was no safer in one place than another, that I will have to explain all of this to my son, that he will have to reconcile who he wants to be with how people will view him and that I will have thoughts of stepping on his freedom and creativity and confidence to keep him safe. That I want nothing more than for him to be brave, but bravery can get him killed. I was enraged. I am enraged. So I kept going, my singular act of defiance. I refused to allow anyone else's fear to move me and my family. I was done with that. I am done with that. I wish I had never done it.

What struck me most that day was how many white faces went out of their way to speak to me. The country was in an uproar. For perhaps one of the first times I saw white people, even some who don't regularly consider themselves allies, yelling for justice. What happened to Ahmaud was somehow too callous even for them. It was hard to understand why this one was the one—not a child like Tamir Rice being shot at the park or Philando Castile being killed while following the precise letter of the law or even Botham Jean being killed in his own home—this one sent outrage. Part of me wondered if it was because we were mid-pandemic. Folks had pent up aggression and emotion and needed a place to put it and this injustice was the vehicle. Or was it that jogging was such a uniquely white pastime? For years white women continued to jog, even after having been warned of the dangers of jogging alone. It was so sacred and so white that New York City was willing to send five teenage Black boys to prison for attacking a white jogger in Central Park despite the evidence that they did not do it, just to make the city feel safe to jog again. In Ahmaud's case the deepest fears of white joggers came to fruition but on a Black body. The first time many could empathize.

On my jog, there were dozens of sidewalk-chalk memorials to Ahmaud. Some in childlike handwriting, others beautifully crafted by some well-intentioned adult whose heart was bleeding today for maybe the first hashtag that ever hit them so hard. I was moved by the children's willingness to speak out in pastel. I was disgusted by the adults. I had walked these streets so many times, my own son in a wagon, followed closely behind by friends or family, through several hashtags and moments of Black despair that encompassed me to the point that even breathing felt too heavy. There was never chalk.

The chalk should have made me feel loved. Welcomed. Supported. Instead, it reminded me of the now dozens of times that I politely choked back my rage or utter hopeless-ness around Xerox machines or debates about Game of Thrones when there was a new report or new hashtag the pre-vious day. There were days that I could barely muster energy to give some fake-ass smile as colleagues asked how my night was, then prattled on about their own, never acknowledging how my night actually might have gone. They would never know how my text messages, phone calls, social media feed lit up in a steady stream of sorrow and terror. How so many friends from all sectors of American industry would congre-gate that night, sometimes just to talk, sometimes just to share space with one another after an exhausting day of pretending everything was fine.

And it wasn't only friends. I was still an assistant when the police shootings in Dallas took place after the BLM rally. I remember watching and crying and being unable to sleep. It felt like everywhere we went that week, every turn we took, there was someone glaring at us, upset that a supposed "peaceful protest" had turned deadly. I hated the bullseye it put on my son's and RJ's heads. As if it were their job to answer for all accusations and actions hurled at every Black man, but no one had to answer for supremacy. But what made me most sad was knowing that no one would ask the right questions. Why had it turned violent? Why were Black folks so angry? So uneasy? So ready to do whatever it takes to taste even a semblance of justice? Why was this justice to us? No one paid attention to our pain or fears. It felt as though we were a people caged, admonished for hurting our captors in our desperate attempts to get free, then being denied freedom for the injury inflicted. Those cages existed everywhere from the steel poles of prisons to the invisible respectability of the modern workplace and neighborhood where even a mention of the gravity of the moment was not acknowledged.

During that week, I made a coffee run for my office. The disillusionment created a daze that I walked through day in and day out. I was functioning. Laughing. On autopilot. But my mind was swirling with the what-ifs. The what-nexts. I walked into the coffee shop and waited in line, watching every white face ahead and behind me discuss something I could not have cared less about—even if I would have cared a few weeks earlier I didn't now. I distinctly remember one couple—perched at a table by the window facing Sunset Boulevard, coffees in hand—discussing the event. They spoke so openly, freely, as if this were a discussion about Mamet or where to go on vacation. The man, looking out of the window to passing cars and a bustling bank across the street uttered words I might never forget:

"What's happening with race in this country is bad. But you can't haul off and shoot someone. I don't know what's going on. This isn't the America I know."

That is when I met the gaze of the only other Black patron. A man, older than me. He must have been in line behind me when I was lost in thought and somehow, we both managed to hear it. We looked at one another. He could read it on my face. The tears stung and while I could blink them back, the glassiness was evident. He saw it and he knew. He shook his head, and half laughed, finally looking back to me. An entire intimate conversation between two strangers in a coffee shop in the middle of Hollywood. No words. Distanced.

No one else saw us. They never do.

As I collected the coffee for the office, I stepped outside and took a deep breath. I could not go back to the workplace tear-stained or feathers ruffled because that would expound the pain. The awkward looks and silences and inability to speak even an iota of life or empathy into my situation, the predicament of every Black person in America that day, would make emotional management all the more difficult. It was better here. On a street, surrounded by strangers with places to be and who owed me nothing, to grasp what I might have left of the day's sanity.

After a few moments, the man from inside stepped out. He had his coffee in hand. Seeing me, he gently placed a hand on my back.

"Be safe out there, sis."

I lost it. I placed the coffees for my office down on the bench beside us and wept. Openly. Loudly. He pulled me in close, a hug from a complete and utter stranger that was somehow also my brother and cousin and confidante, and let me cry. No one stopped us. No one looked our way. The world seemed to continue to stride by, as if we were merely trees planted in the pavement for the enjoyment of their shade on sunny days, little other than a fixture to color their world. I caught my breath. I couldn't look up at him out of embarrassment. I quickly gathered the coffees I had placed down.

"I'm sorry."

"It's been a tough week. Take care of yourself."

We glanced at each other then. I don't remember his face and I wonder if I ever will. Another forced smile that would lead into another and another for the rest of the day. For the rest of our lives. I returned to work. Returned to the thin veil of normalcy that was necessary in all white spaces. No one responded to the deaths that had preceded that moment. There was no public outcry or understandable rage. There was silence. There were forward stares as two Black folks held each other and cried on one of the busiest streets in Los Angeles. There was certainly no chalk.

The colorful chalk on the Larchmont Village pavement was meant, in its purest form, to comfort people like me. To let us know that we belong and are needed and are cherished. The point was for us to know that we are seen. Our pain is heard and our lives matter. But I had been on that pavement. My Black body had stood on concrete connected to this only a mile or so away. It had stood, broken and weeping, and been virtually ignored by every face that passed except for one: another Black face. As companies changed their social media profiles and released statements about their distress over the death of Ahmaud and how they were committed to "amplifying" Black voices and "anti-racism," my own voice had been drowned out by the hum of an espresso machine. Chalk like this infuriated me.

It wasn't that I didn't welcome the attempts. Or the calls and texts I received from so many, offering their support and even their apologies for not having been so supportive before. In many ways, I felt the criticism of folks who did that unfair. Never had privilege been discussed the way it had been in the past decade. No one had ever been forced to sit and consider their thoughts and lifestyle more than they had in 2020, cooped up in homes for months because of the pandemic. Never had folks had as much time to read, had such instant access to digestible bites of outside thought (and misinformation). The moment was unprecedented. I have been in therapy for the better part of my life and so have many people I love and what we all know is that being faced with a character flaw or defect and meeting it with apology and willingness to attempt change is no easy feat. That was never lost on me. That was not what I considered performative. Those were not the people I considered performative. I didn't even feel as though the sudden outrage was performative when it quietly stopped and dripped into another hot button issue like the virus or the upcoming presidential elections or climate change. For Black folks, we are Black before everything else.

Racism trumps all those things because it is an assault on our very personhood. Our lives. The same was true for the border crisis. The same was true for LGBTQ issues. The same was true for families suffering from COVID. There was no point in comparing or trying to quickly determine that someone "didn't mean" their empathy or compassion if after a week of posting or showing grief they moved on to another topic. The world was on fire. There was a lot to consider, to fight, and so many lives were at stake.

What felt performative to me were the multi-million-dollar homes with chalk on the sidewalk and signs for their children's schools in the lawn—some of the most prestigious and elite schools in the area. These signs had become the replacement celebration for otherwise-normal graduations, since quarantine had rendered it impossible. Preschool to kindergarten. Elementary to middle school. Middle to high school. Yard signs were sprinkled all throughout the neighborhood as children toddled their way to a new chapter of life trapped in homes and behind screens. The juxtaposition of the chalk outside so many of these homes and homes like them was what felt wrong. The access inside each and every one of these homes that allowed them to pay tens of thousands of dollars in property taxes but deem the local public schools "not good enough." The bulldozing of old multi-family homes and the clearing of local haunts to create shopping centers and modern apartment buildings, displacing all the Black and brown bodies that had lived there before and who now could no longer afford the streets they grew up on. The brazen "there is someone very

suspicious walking up and down the street" in the neighborhood chat groups. A consistent and constant dismissal of the
Black lives around them. But bubble letters perfectly scripted
on the concrete outside of their homes begged me to believe
they "saw me."

They had never seen me. The hundreds of walks in this
neighborhood. The days racing up and down the sidewalk with
my son. The hours stopping in front of homes, checking for
sale signs, calculating what I would have to make—what I
would have to *do*—to be able to purchase a home even close to
this place. The fear of lingering too long, worried that someone
may think that I and whomever I might be walking with that
day were casing the place. The fear that I wished Ahmaud had
lest he still be alive but a fear that no one with a dream should
ever have to consider—will they find my dreaming a threat?
They didn't see me. They saw him in Georgia. Shot him for
seeing him. But they never saw me.

That anger pushed me to continue my jog. To not say hello.
To not greet a single face who attempted to offer even the
smallest bit of solace in their smile. My steps were heavy.
There was no rhythm or sync to the way my feet hit each step.
I was just trying to make it to the end. To finish the race. To
get to the edge my neighborhood and my own personal
despair and allow God to decide which would collapse first:
my body or my spirit.

I never would have done this in the Crenshaw district. I
would not have had to. I would have lamented the loss to RJ.
When I took the garbage cans outside the old woman across
the street would have asked me if I had heard of the story and

offered her thoughts. The musician a few houses down would have surely had something to contribute to the conversation as would every face at the local grocery store or pharmacy or restaurant. There would have been no apologies or feigned ignorance to "just how bad it was." Instead we would have shared stories. Friends. Cousins. Brothers. Our own lives when we were met with similar circumstances and neared similar fates to Ahmaud. We would have told stories from our hometowns and communities, ones that rarely made the news, that mirrored the moment, all but forgotten in the public relocation but still weighed on our hearts and minds and perceptions of the world as heavily as they did the day they happened. Perhaps heavier on days like this. No one would be running and posting on social media in an effort to show solidarity, we *were* solidarity. Solidarity was us. We were each other's unifying force.

The irony was that a white woman jogging could change all of that with her mere existence. A white woman jogger was more of a threat on 78th Place than a Black man jogging in Georgia could ever be. But only one was killed.

I turned into a part of the neighborhood that I knew well. My old boss owned a home in the eastern section and before I had ever moved here, I would frequent the area. Running errands and coming for dinner were normal, but what had truly made me a fan of Larchmont Village and prompted us to move there after RJ and I divorced was Halloween. We started the tradition on my son's first Halloween at my old boss's urging. His children—both dangerously close to not wanting to trick-or-treat anymore—had grown up going door to door in the neighborhood and it was one of the single moments of childhood that even they were reluctant to let go as they entered their teenage years. Larchmont is one of the few mostly flat neighborhoods in Mid-Wilshire and has a few square miles of close-together homes that are affluent, picturesque, and give a true sense of neighborhood. People flock to the area—some from nearby Koreatown or Pico Robertson where there are mostly large apartment buildings and duplexes, some people like us, from completely different parts of Los Angeles, who heard from someone else that the bounty was in Larchmont.

What was better about the neighborhood is that they prepared. They didn't scoff at the droves of children who came to trick-or-treat. They knew these weren't children from their own community. The sheer number of tiny princesses and Marios and vampires was a clear indication that there were outsiders. There weren't thousands of homes to house the thousands of kids that wove their way on and off of lawns and doorsteps. But the demographic made it clearer. Every race, ethnicity, and culture would be represented in those trick-or-treaters. Some spoke no English. Some went to school together. All parents talked to one another. It was not uncommon to catch a waddling two-year-old as she almost toppled off of a curb, top-heavy from a pumpkin costume, while her mother dashed over, thanking you for breaking her fall as she tried to catch up. If there was a game on, some doors would be swung wide open so dads trick-or-treating with their kids could catch a glimpse and update from the dad furiously throwing out candy to the witches knocking.

The candy never stopped flowing. The neighbors never seemed upset that their community was overrun. They decorated. They set out patio furniture. They took pictures. One family set up a cotton candy station every year. Larchmont made Halloween feel like a warm hug from the city. Like your neighbors liked you.

We celebrated there every year after. My boss was no longer my boss by the day I ran. He was one of my best friends. His daughters were no longer trick-or-treating, but they would always wait before going to their high school Halloween parties to see my son off. We started in a stroller and now my son ran with his friends from school. But some things remained constant: The texts the week before to make sure the "tradition still stood." The ordering of pizza for my kid's arrival. The changing into costumes in the kitchen. Then off into the neighborhood for its embrace. Maybe that's why I turned down the street that day. We were months away from Halloween, but it's the only place I could remember feeling totally welcomed outside of Crenshaw, even if only once a year.

It was there that I stopped jogging. I walked. I panted heavily, too out of shape to even attempt what I had but moving on pure adrenaline. I hadn't felt the burning of my calves or the throbbing of my soles until now. By then my jog was barely more than a walk and somehow, crossing Larchmont Boulevard and making it to the more eastern side made me feel more at ease. Like I could rest there. This side was arguably more affluent than the other. The houses were bigger. The school signs more abundant. But there wasn't chalk.

Instead, there were flags. There were huge pieces of cardboard taped to trees and hurriedly scribbled on. Quickly. Urgently. They hung from balcony windows like revolutionary ribbons.

BLM

NO ONE SHOULD BE KILLED FOR JOGGING.

I remember stopping altogether a few blocks over and looking at one such sign. A bed sheet, spray painted with black spray paint. The sheet must have been for a California King. It felt enormous. Sand-colored. Crumpled. It took up a good portion of the front of a multi-million-dollar home. In bold letters, only possible by an adult, it read BLACK LIVES MATTER. What I didn't know then is that only a week or two later they would add "DEFUND THE POLICE" to that sheet. The video of George Floyd dying would be released and the city would protest for weeks. But that day, it stopped me. It was the only thing that did.

I wished the owners would come out so I could see them. They didn't. But I stood. And looked, gawked really, at the bedsheet tethered outside of this estate. No one had taken time to make it beautiful, or painstakingly centered the wording or ironed the linen. They had never considered the eye-sore it might be in a neighborhood like this. Or maybe they did and didn't care. It seemed no one on the street cared, because there were so many ragtag signs like this, but this was the largest and most beautiful of all. It blocked a downstairs window. I don't know what room it was, but it undoubtedly obstructed views and diminished the light that could filter into the house. That didn't matter to whomever did this, there was an urgent message—a line they had to draw in the sand—and it couldn't wait for eloquence or an ordered flag from a website or for the forty-five minutes it might take to fill the word "Black" with pastel purple chalk only to be washed away when the sprinklers came on that night. They needed to say something for the world to know, for every passerby that knew the owners of that home to associate that phrase with them. To know they stood by it. To say they were willing to "lose" aesthetically, to sacrifice even the smallest piece of their personal privilege to stand by. They locked arms with the kids who knocked on their door every October 31st. They replaced the giant inflatable skeletons that made the little Black and brown faces—my son being one of them—squeal and replaced it with a sign that plainly told the world those faces mattered to them.

Weeks later even those gestures would seem performative. People so quickly learned what to say and do and what to look like to appear as though they were for humanity. Folks I know who would proudly defend the actions of any perpetrator in any of the hashtag videos we saw summer 2020 were also blacking out their social media profiles in solidarity. A sign on a lawn would never be enough again. But for that week it was. And that day, before it became a popular artifice of a supposed awakening, that sign in that yard on that sheet made all the difference. It allowed me to stop jogging. To stop walking. To stop toiling. It allowed me to openly mourn. Not to push back or down for the sake of polite company or "normalcy." I didn't flock to kinfolk whom I knew would understand. But there on that Larchmont sidewalk, I wailed.

The tears burned coming down my face. The saltiness of my sweat and anguish streamed into my mouth, every single breath was audible. Exhaustion from the running. Exhaustion from the running. Both. It was not like the coffee shop that day. There were no people outside, the pandemic having swept us all indoors save a few early morning walkers here and there. Should anyone had been outside, they couldn't have embraced me the way the man did that day for the same reason. There was a deep loneliness attached to it all. But also a comfort in knowing that here, for these few blocks, when they couldn't hug you they would shout their love out. If you couldn't feel them, you would see them. That sign offered the head nod, the acknowledgement, the "I see you" that the white woman jogger had never offered. This whole street said "hello" to my Black face. It always had.

I walked home.

* * *

THE DEATH OF GEORGE FLOYD WEEKS later set LA ablaze. The air was so thick, the city a powder keg. Every day, despite the deadliness of the virus we knew so little about, thousands of protestors would pass by our balcony. I made my son make signs and had them waiting by the door. When we heard them coming, we would drop everything and stand up with our signs and wave at the protestors, throwing water and fruit snacks and whatever we might have down to them below. Everyday my son would beg to go walk with them. I feared for his health and safety. He was so tiny, and the LAPD was not being discerning about their rubber bullets. My friend Deon had just had his skull fractured by a rubber bullet a week earlier and stories were pouring in of even children being pepper sprayed. My son's lungs were already compromised and couldn't handle either COVID or trauma and it seemed irresponsible to allow him so close to so much danger. It also seemed irresponsible to not teach him to fight for his people or his freedom or join the movement despite fear.

After days of protests, I loaded him into the car and got ahead of the protestors. We parked across the street and I allowed him to march parallel to them, but it wasn't good enough for him. He wanted to be where they were. I prayed silently as we crossed over Vine street, welling with pride at such a bold and beautiful little person while desperately calculating where I would run him to safety if things went left. They didn't. He stood and marched for about a quarter mile. He wanted to continue but the protestors were marching directly into the zone now covered by the National Guard and I never wanted those images in his mind. We left Crenshaw because of the brutalization of Black bodies and I drew my line there. Until he could understand every nuance, the history, I never wanted him to fear these moments. Only to beg his mama to join them.

Those National Guard tanks moved closer and closer to Larchmont until a week or two later they were parked on the Boulevard, in the parking lot formerly occupied every Sunday by the local Farmer's Market, now shuttered. They marched up and down the street. Patrolling I don't know what. The protestors never really made it into Larchmont. The police ensured that, heavily barricading and violently pushing them back to

ensure the rich people's homes were not devastated in the protests. The Mayor's home was also in the vicinity. The blocks
surrounding Eric Garcetti's owned-by-the-city-of-Los-Angeles
home were blocked off. The man who the people elected didn't
want the people close to him or questioning him about his
stance on police or the National Guard.

Our walks stopped when the National Guard came to
Larchmont. White joggers still ran. I watched them from my
window daily. But we stopped walking. One warm morning
when a group of older residents who regularly congregated
around the Peet's Coffee at the end of the block thanked the
Guard for being here, myself and a few others openly argued
with them about their remarks. We were told to "get over it."
If we didn't like how things were going, "we could leave."
There was little reason to continue. I didn't want my son to
see the tanks. Or those people. I didn't want them offering
even a cordial "hello" to him knowing they considered his
walk a threat. They rarely said hello anyway. People like that
don't see us.

When I arrived home after that incident, I spoke to RJ, who
was quarantining with us, about whether this was a safe place
to raise our son. Nothing actually felt safe then. Nowhere feels
safe now. But he brought up the homes we saw early on.
Specifically the one with the bedsheet.

"You deserve to live wherever you want," he said. "You can
fly whatever flag you want in front of your house. It's yours.
And you know there are people here that would support you."

"Yes, but there are also people here who would gladly have
us locked up or make us leave," I replied.

"They don't get to tell us shit. That's the point of all of this. This is ours too. They don't get to tell us where we can be."

I watched my son protest from the balcony that night. We ate on the balcony. Talked. Stayed on the balcony until we were all full and sleepy. My mind churned about the day. The week. The year. The videos I had seen. The videos I wished I hadn't. I wondered where we could go. Where was home? Where could we ever be, anywhere, that didn't carry a soft hum of warning about being too this or too that. Was there anywhere we could be—can be—that would be entirely ours. Could we even afford it if there was? Was there any place safe?

I watched as a young white woman crossed Melrose in sneakers and a sports bra. She might not have been jogging. Maybe she was just dressed like that. It was LA after all. But I instinctively knew that if this is where she felt safe to be, this might not be the place in the city for us.

SEVEN

TEXTS WITH CHAZ

Chaz,

The me you remember is not who I am now. The me you remember was young. And brave. Ideological. Full of youthful exuberance and a belief that was nearly cellular that my friends and I would change the world. You are my friend. My dear friend. So I know you remember that me.

She is gone. She died in November 2015. She died after eighteen hours of labor, twenty minutes of pushing, and the loudest, sweetest, most heartbreaking cry her ears had ever heard. The moment I became a mother, I became fierce and frightened. I didn't experience the "instant love" everyone talks about. My body was traumatized, my mind still dazed. My pregnancy wasn't easy and this small thing, though my feelings towards it could not be described as anything but obsessed, had been parasitical to my body and seemed foreign to me. It took two entire calendar weeks before I had the visceral sense of love everyone swore would happen the moment I held him. But immediately, from the moment I laid eyes on him, my most animalistic instincts kicked in. And I knew I would die for him.

I watched the doctors handle him gently and bring him to the warming table where his father would cut the umbilical cord. My hands began to shake because I couldn't see him. I worried how they might be handling him. If their grasp was too rough. I knew his Daddy was there, but I didn't care. I had to know for myself. I kept asking, through sewing of the tears his giant body had inflicted upon me:

"Is he okay?"

Everyone assured me he was. Some laughed at how clingy "mama" already was. But it wasn't love. Not yet. It was a guttural instinct to keep him safe.

He gave me two stitches. A resident worked on me and I felt every incision. I never flinched. My fear was that the medical staff would try and comfort me and in doing so obstruct my view of the warming table. I never even said it hurt. I was afraid they'd stand up and his foot would be out of view. His foot was all I could see, and I convinced myself that none of his ten-minute-old flailing was random. If even a toe moved the wrong way, I would be able to sense distress.

That's when I knew I was dead.

You've known me as an organizer. A staffer. A leader. You've seen me as a young woman speaking (mostly yelling) to anyone that would listen about oppression. Black lives. Injustice. We marched together for Martin Anderson. Trayvon. We wrote together on everything in-between and everything after. You've watched me make giant missteps in my thinking—for the revolution and personally. You've watched me bounce back. You've seen me grow into the woman I was before that November. A woman who would likely lay down her life and all her ambitions for those most vulnerable, for people in need, for people whose voices couldn't be heard.

Now my life belongs to that tiny foot. Should I leave him too long, I leave him vulnerable and in need. I am his voice.

Chaz, I am terrified. Perpetually.

The fire that burns in the pit of my stomach when I see a Black life lost or disregarded or even disrespected has grown as a mother. I remember us, as young activists, saying, "This could be our sons. Our daughters. Our siblings. This could be us!" But I didn't have a son or daughter then. I didn't know the way a hashtag could ignite that flame in my innermost self. It used to be that a new incident would send me to a word processor, or to emails to see where we were mobilizing. *Who* was mobilizing. I would breathe fire, sparks in eyes, and shoot it from my fingertips until exhausted. I was in constant search of a remedy for supremacy and a pathway to freedom.

I assumed that having a child would make that flame grow. I did. My assumption was that I would drag him to every strategy meeting and townhall. That he would be the protest baby and stare National Guardsman in the eye, unafraid just like his mama. But how I thought I would be . . . I'm not.

That fire now consumes me. It scorches my heart. I feel the burning so intensely that I want to double over. I would drink something cool if I thought my hands wouldn't shatter the glass. Before becoming a mother, I cried a lot. Sappy movies. Physical pain. Hurt feelings. I cried about everything except in the Revolution. There I was steadfast. Now it's the inverse. I rarely shed tears outside of major childhood milestones and fearfulness for my son's health, well-being, or future. I cry.

Uncontrollably. Heaves. Now the Revolution makes me cry. Because every hashtag was a baby and every baby has a mother and, God be with us, that pain.

That fire no longer spits from my fingers or shoots from my words. It burns in my heart. I gasp for air as the smoke fills my lungs. I can't imagine this person—some mother's child—taking their last breath. Or the air that must have left that woman's lungs when someone had to tell her that her baby was gone. I think of Sybrina. Oh, Chaz. Sybrina. I cry for her every time. My legs feel charred from the inside. Burnt to a crisp. Wobbly and paralyzed. I can't move. I can't think. I can't do anything but watch both the news and the little body on the floor shooting imaginary spiderwebs from his veins, the hero of his tiny world, with visions of being able to save the world he's in one day. One that is burning. And justifying murders of people like him.

The fire that once blasted me off now cripples me. I still take him to every town hall and strategy meeting I attend. But I attend them with far less frequency. How can I come home and provide him a safe haven, away from judgement and pre-conceived notions about his skin and personhood, a place of freedom to live fully as himself if I am on fire? How can I help him put together a puzzle when my cremated fingers ash onto a dizzyingly bright picture of a lion and gazelle loving one another harmoniously in a twenty-four-piece jungle?

But how can I not allow myself to be consumed? Who will save my son but me? But us? And the mothers who have found a way to let the person they've birthed fuel their work: Tamika. Patrisse. Mrs. Edelman. They can do it. You are doing it. Since your daughter was born you have not relented. You've almost become more precise. More laser focused. I read every paper. Every study. I beam with pride. And then I wonder. How are you doing it? How are any of you doing it? I can hide behind my art. I don't know how to write or create from an inauthentic place so the Revolution will always be in my work. And I can always say that. But I'm not doing the work organizationally anymore. Not like you all. In part, it feels like it's because that chapter is over. My platform now is with a pen. Dialogue or prose. This is mine now. But that is only one part.

The other part is because I'm too damn scared. Too scared to put my baby in the line of fire directly or indirectly. Too scared not to for fear that he never experiences freedom. Or worse, that he never learns that it is his duty to fight for freedom for others. He will undoubtedly learn that from my own actions. So, I go. But only in part. Half of me is still melted into a chair somewhere, praying for mercy for myself and my son.

No one answers.

How are you doing this Chaz? Do you ever feel this feeling? What broke inside of me? Why can't I fix it?

—*VBK*

* * *

Chaz,

It makes me sad too, friend.

I took so much painstaking care in deciding where Ryder and I would live after the divorce. A place that feels economically viable, has funded schools and grocery options, an uncomplicated relationship with the city, and secure outdoor spaces, but also has enough Black people in and around it that you don't feel like a unicorn is hard to come by in Los Angeles. In America, really. I drool over Baldwin Hills and Ladera Heights. Windsor Hills. Inglewood. I wish we could go back. But white flight pushed resources out of those areas. They are still one half of the equation, but not the other. Even though that is where my heart is, to survive alone with my son, and with very little help elsewhere, I'm in Larchmont. That same conundrum pushed me to choose a private school. Betsy DeVos took office, and I knew that anywhere we could afford to buy a home would be criminally underfunded. It was the hardest decision of my life, and it is the persistent moral issue of this moment.

Do I stay and fight and risk my child for the greater good or do I fight to get us both into the places and spaces they try to keep us from? Infiltrate from within. I used to think the latter was safer. It's not. To some degree you have to be complicit to work from the inside. I am having trouble even formulating my thoughts in this correspondence. It doesn't feel like anything is safe.

I want to be clear with you that when I say "safe," I don't mean physical danger. I never worried for my life the way the news and televisions like to portray the Black and brown areas of the city. I can't be certain, but I'm sure you understand. Recently I dropped off cupcakes to you and your wife. I left them hanging on the doorknob of your outside gate. I didn't tell you I was coming. I didn't tell anyone. Instead, that day Ryder and I ordered four dozen cupcakes from a Black-owned bakery (a FAMU alum, might I add) and left them on the doorsteps of our friends and family here in Los Angeles. We missed you all during the pandemic. It was not yet safe—it is still not yet safe at the time of this writing—to touch or hug or break bread together. So we sent our love through confections. We typed up messages to each person and Ryder would run to their door, leave the cupcake, then jump back into the backseat of my car. Your house was so far from the gate we texted to let you know there was a gift for you outside.

By the time you saw that text and arrived at your gate it was gone.

Neither of us seemed upset. (I wasn't. I didn't think you were either.) We knew the neighborhood you were living in at that moment was one that had been robbed of resources for some time. I don't even think we used the word "stole." The cupcakes were just "gone." And we talked about how someone came upon some amazing pastries. Still you lived there, with your wife and child. I dropped cupcakes off, drove through and past. And that was just life.

Inglewood was similar for me. My ex's mother sent us a bunch of things for the baby when I was pregnant. She took the box from her brand-new vacuum and stuffed it to the brim with onesies and bottles and everything imaginable for our son. I never received it. She checked the post office. The tracking number. It had been delivered and left on our porch. That was the information we needed. It was "lost to the streets." A few days later, my neighbor knocked with a bottle cleaner and bib in her hand. She asked if they were mine. I explained what happened and her face went stoic. She nodded, and assured me everything that my mother-in-law sent would be returned promptly. Every day, she piecemealed that box back together. One day some bottles. The next few some socks, still packaged. After a few more days I told her not to worry about it. If it was taking her this long, she was having to go to several different houses, meaning the booty of my son's package had been parceled out amongst several. It was a luxury for us but a necessity for them—one I would have gladly handed over had I known. Now I did. They could have it.

Parcels being taken was my greatest fear. I didn't fear for my safety or that of my family by the hands of the neighborhood. I would be lying if I said there weren't certain areas that I would not have been so comfortable in. Areas never rebuilt from the '91 Uprising. Places the city left behind—unincorporated and underfunded because that is where we were. There are pockets of the city almost unofficially set aside for mental illness and folks without homes. For neglect. The interesting part is the news doesn't even show those areas. The crews themselves are too frightened to go there and the government at large doesn't want their images out. It would be a blemish on leadership. Instead we pretend they don't exist.

What they show the world is where we lived. It's deemed dangerous because there are gangs and shootings and all of these buzzwords that make folks fearful of Black bodies. They leave out that there are more crimes in Hollywood and Downtown Los Angeles than Leimert Park. I'm more fearful to walk alone on a side street in Hollywood at night than I ever was in my old neighborhood. That is never what I meant by "safe."

We were unsafe because South LA is always a target. If there is money needed for something, pull it out of the budget that helps South LA's schools. If we want to bolster money for the police, point to South LA as the necessity for a greater police force. If you want to cover the need for better health care or cleaner streets, by all means ignore Venice, where we rely on tourism but it's littered to the hilt. Come to Slauson and Crenshaw. South LA has been the place they "make an example of." The place people certainly do not send their children to public school—both for reasons founded and unfounded—and one of the only places we could live where we could step out of our homes and feel at home.

The constant PR-pounding South LA takes has taken its toll. That sort of blatant racism depletes a place. It could never rob it of its humanity, Black folk are far too resilient for that, but it robs it of its resources. And resources are finite. When I worked at Community Coalition, I would listen to the young people sometimes discuss having to cross neighborhoods. The safety of their block was one thing, but to walk to and from school meant to walk into blocks that may be hostile to an outsider. That sometimes meant fighting. Other times, intimidation. But it was a reality for them. They didn't hate anyone from any other neighborhood. They understood the feeling. No one comes to or through these parts of Los Angeles without a reason. They were discarded by the system. On their own. The neighborhood was on guard to see what your reason might be: were you a friend or foe? Some folks wouldn't wait to find out. I benefited from that in my own neighborhood. From knowing that my block would protect me. But we could just as easily fall victim to it blocks away. In the case of my kid, he could fall victim to it every day.

We had to make a decision, Chaz. Could we stand to leave our son in the midst of this? We knew we could fight and be at every PTA meeting and every rally and stand behind every candidate who was working to fix this broken-ass system. We would do that. We would fight diligently. But we had been fighting this fight for decades. Long before our arrival to Los Angeles County. Long before our birth. Making headway was one thing. But fixing anything . . . that felt fruitless. Years ago, we knew we had to tear the thing down for it to ever be built up again. We knew that in Tallahassee. It seemed, however awful you might think me, that staying was to stay in a sinking ship. We would forever be funneling water over the side, sometimes our buckets large enough to gain some reprieve only to watch it slowly seeping through cracks and rotted planks moments later. The only recourse was to convince those on board with us to dismantle what we stood on, while simultaneously building something out of what remained. Or abandon ship.

When folks are trying not to drown, no one has time to logically work through the "how to build a new boat" manual. They were not interested in dismantling. There were not enough people prepared to do the work necessary to make that plan work. They kept tossing buckets of seawater overboard. They still are.

We put on our life vests and swam.

There is guilt there. It penetrates deeply. The concern that we should have stayed and convinced everyone, or at least tried to help grant some respite. But when I would consider what that meant for my son—whose life was mine to care for and who owned me—it became impossible. Even in writing this I wonder why I never thought then what I'm thinking now: why did I feel like it was my burden to carry? Why did I blame myself for not staying as opposed to blaming the people who gave my community a broken boat? Who refused to equip them with materials to sustain it? Who put them out to sea? I fell into the very American trap of allowing capitalism to rob me, then guilt me for being broke but offer to help me out of my precarious situation for a nominal fee.

I never thought that moving would solve every problem. In fact, I knew it would carry with it a new set of issues. Maybe better. Maybe worse. I didn't know. But we had to find out. At the bare minimum it seemed that some relief would follow when I knew lack of resources, a matter I had no control over, was not plaguing those around us. That diffuses so much. I remembered the anxiety of not knowing how I would pay my bills. Not knowing where rent was coming from. Even when I wasn't thinking about it, it played in the background like unknown music in some browser that has one hundred open tabs, each its own worry. And that music plays. And you can't find it and you can't stop it, and it's heavy and irritating, and it etches at your patience. Soon you are edgy, day ruined, worn to a nub, and it can all be traced to that damn music that kept a steady hum all day. Even when you close your computer, it's too late. You're worn out. That's what can happen to our people. That's what can happen to us when we are consistently withheld resources.

I thought I could, at minimum, lose that stress. And I did. But the new one I gained was not lighter. It was not easier to carry. In some ways it was an even exchange. In other ways it felt worse because at least in our own communities we can speak freely. We have a shorthand with one another that no one needs to explain themselves or where they are coming from. Even if we disagree, we disagree in the same language. There, in a whiter world where resources abounded, supremacy reigned. It was never how I imagined it would be, or even how I had seen it when we were in the South. Here it was different. It was the clothes you wore, your cadence. The car you drove, the things you did. All the things you had to do to show you had some deeply entrenched understanding of whiteness. Just below the surface of that— but barely—was the troublesome reality that whiteness only existed by othering. These communities, the safety and resource, only existed, by othering. So should an "other" come here, it was not our job to advocate for the "other" (ourselves included). It was to enjoy the bounty of whiteness. Disturbing that whiteness—calling to attention bigotry, racism, entitlement—called out the very thing that allowed this safe haven to exist. And it was frowned upon. You'd be isolated. Shunned.

How do you advocate for your child in that space? How do you tell his teachers that he is judged more harshly? That he is treated differently? That his history is not being taught here and his identity is not wrapped up in his proximity to them? How do you not allow him to be tokenized?

Tokenized or weaponized. It feels like we have no choices.

You know me. And well. If I marched on capitols and organized civil disobediences, there was no way Caucasia would scare me from advocating for my son. I picked up our lives and left my community to come here; they were going to treat us fairly. I could not have cared less if they didn't like me or looked at me scathingly for disrupting their supremacy. We were coming for what not only was rightly ours but should be available to all of our folks.

I never bargained for what it would feel like when the disapproval of your advocacy stretches to your child. I was in no way prepared for anyone to treat him differently, or even like a problem, because his mother demands his equal and fair treatment. I had kind of felt that feeling before. It was on the proverbial boat, trying to convince others to burn and dismantle it. There was always an alienation there, but there was company. No one thought it wrong, merely not possible. Here, speaking loudly and candidly made us pariahs. It called forth the fact that we didn't belong here. This place was not made for us.

The entire topic makes my head spin. It makes me both woozy and nauseous and I lose the ability to think rationally about anything. It feels like the weight of the world drops on me and I stand like Atlas, trying to stop it from collapsing. The casualties being my son and your daughter and everyone I love.

I'm terrified.

—*Vanessa*

* * *

Chaz,

Thank you for being you. For being someone I can run these questions by without judgment or reprieve. I'm more grateful for relationships like ours now than ever before. Mostly because of the isolation I have felt in parenting, and in general.

I've worked hard to find other Black parents to connect with in the city. I swore growing up that I would never join an elitist organization like Jack and Jill or something so niche as Mocha Moms when I became a parent. Instead I would work tirelessly to keep a solid foundation of friends and like-minded neighbors and "cousins" like your daughter around so that my son's community would be in place and I would have no excuse for another group membership as opposed to doing the work of placing my kid in Black spaces.

Two years into parenthood and we were in Jack and Jill. I wouldn't even admit it to some of our mutual friends. The organization has such a problematic reputation and past that I couldn't bear it. But we were isolated. And I was scared. I was three thousand miles away from all of my college friends. You had yet to arrive and your daughter was not even imagined yet. I was desperate.

I came to find that so was every other mother in the Pasadena Chapter of Jack and Jill. Living in Glendale, that was where I was assigned and where I have stayed even as I moved into LA. I petitioned to stay because of the women there. They were nothing like the mothers I had seen in the organization growing up. These were not women who found their daughters physically unacceptable without bone straight hair and skin lighter than a paper bag, nor were they interested in debutantes or status. (Well, some were interested in status. We are in LA.) These were women whose children were in white spaces and who needed sisterhood to help them get buck when they needed to. And they needed to a lot.

Within my first year of Jack and Jill, those mothers had helped me confront discrimination at my son's school, advocate for my son with his doctor (which eventually turned into my moving him to a Black woman pediatrician elsewhere), and so much more. They were woke and natural-haired and in many ways revolutionaries. In some ways I wasn't prepared for.

Several mothers in my chapter were gun owners and sharp shooters and proud of such. They had abandoned nonviolence as the only way to reach equality. There were actually quite a few who didn't believe in it at all. All of them cited their children's births as the catalyst of their shifts from the Civil Rights era beliefs that freedom is won through nonviolent resistance and civil disobedience. They still believed in disruption of the system, that was why many chose to send their children to the schools they were in and live in the neighborhoods they did. They wanted the lily-white neighbors of Pasadena to walk outside and see their Black-ass faces and Black-ass families, smell their barbeque and not be able to say a damn thing to 'em. In that, they also recognized the necessity to protect their families. To protect their children from the "carrying" of those neighbors. Some who, we so recently discovered, may shoot their child should he decide to jog in his neighborhood. These women decided that they wanted to be on offense. They were tired of being in a defensive posture—hashtagging their babies and begging people through rallies to not allow their deaths to be in vain. They would rather take their chances: take out the bigot ("get them before they get us") and take their chances on rallying behind the hypocrisy of self-defense for the Black body. At worst they might be jailed, but everyone that mattered would still be alive and their voices still able to rise.

I love those mothers. I love them deeply. But I'm not there yet. Maybe I am not radical enough. Maybe they will get me there. Maybe I'm just so perpetually terrified that the better plan to me is to keep my son at my side and use my body as his shield. Or run. I feel like as a parent I am somehow always running now. My fight-or-flight instinct was never this. It was always fight. Now it is to survive. Is this what parenthood is like for you? Are you more of a Pasadena Jack and Jill Mama than me?

Can you even believe I am saying that sentence?

—*Vanessa*

* * *

CHAZ,

Did you know that one of the lesser-known inciting incidents of the rise of the Nazi party and World War II was the assassination of German diplomat Ernst vom Rath? You probably do know that because you know so much. I find myself monitoring your posts, your work, your texts—asking you questions only moments after I've asked myself. The diplomat was killed by a sixteen-year-old Jewish boy named Herschel Grynszpan. Herschel was already radicalized. Germany had been showing disdain for the Jewish population. Hitler gave voice to an underbelly of polite culture that hated Jews but found it impolite to say so. Not only did he make it okay to speak that hate publicly, he pushed the conversation further in that he blamed the entirety of Germany's financial issues, crime problems, and utter demise (problems entirely of their own making after waging the first World War) on anyone of Jewish descent.

Herschel was angry at how the Nazi party treated Jews—how he was treated in school and on the streets, and the way the Nazi party spoke about them in public forums. He decided he would take matters into his own hands. He would be a revolutionary. He would strike. His killing of the diplomat—understandable but misguided anger—was used by Nazis as a battle cry to wage war on both Poland and Jews. A teenager became some human decoupage to dress up a political party's ambitions to rule the world and exterminate anyone they believed to be of lower class. The declaration of war on Poland started WWII.

I fear that for us daily.

The streets are burning now as we speak. I waited before going out to the protests. Not for any real reason but mostly to see where folks ended up. I texted Alberto Retana to see if he had brought his children with him to the rally. I never imagined the texts that I would receive back. They were short, to the point: do not bring kids. He left his own at home and was happy that he had. The police officers were agitating the crowd. Moments later it was violent. He was leaving. Then the smoke plume from Fairfax rose just high enough in the sky that it could be seen from my balcony. I was certain the city was on fire. I rushed to my television while simultaneously checking social media. The now-famous photo of a charred LAPD cruiser in the middle of Fairfax and Beverly was everywhere.

I instantly found that so curious. The police started it. I was talking to Alberto as it happened. I watched it in real time on Kendrick's page. They swung. Shot. Taunted. They kept doing it, urging a response. And when anyone swung back, they were given license to shoot. They were "justified." The names and culture and dates change but totalitarianism never does. Fascism never does. Bigotry and hate stay the same in and out of time. So many Herschels that day. So many.

I want to be on board with the idea that carrying and defending ourselves with our "God Given 2nd Amendment Rights" is the answer. But I saw what they did. What they did to Herschel. To Trayvon. To Philando. In a system that is not created for us to have any equal treatment, it is, by my summations, unwise to believe that the most cherished and dangerous of all the constitutional rights would be equally bestowed upon us either. To think that we would ever "defend" ourselves and not be met with a barrage of bullets is crazy. Fred Hampton met that fate. So many in the Panther Party saw the same. History has a way of forewarning us of what is to come. I can't ignore that.

I've heard so many say that if death is inevitable, they would like to know they went down defending their families. As we speak there are tanks on my block. Under my window last week, LAPD rode in military formation—at minimum one hundred officers—to receive protestors on Sunset Boulevard who, at that point, were doing nothing but marching. They were in full swat regalia: two armed rifles and God knows how many handguns apiece. Kevlar everything. In the words of Lin Manuel, we are outgunned. Outmanned. Outnumbered.

Outplanned. The bravado of thinking we could storm them, take out a few and kiss our loved ones goodbye before martyring ourselves as our families flee to safety is frankly a Hollywood movie. I write them. I know.

Instead they will drop bombs on us like Philadelphia or Tulsa. They will "raid" our homes and shoot us in our sleep like Chairman Hampton. They will shoot us with our hands up. I feel like we have to be smarter than this. We have to resist the urge to meet fire with fire because that is not what is happening. We have fire. They have napalm. It all burns, sure, but one is a far more viscous, long-lasting killer that kills beyond its initial impact and holds such a slim chance of recovery that even if you should survive, you'd wish you died. Our resources are not the same. Carrying may make us feel good. As though we have some chance, some means of protection. From a thirty-thousand-foot view, it seems like we are children grasping for our security blankets and hoping our teddies will save us under an aerial attack. Vigilante justice—Proud Boys and rednecks who want to hurt us—sure. Those will protect us from them. Kind of. They will still have the upper hand in a court of law but at least you leave with your life. But that is not who I fear. I fear the police state. The system.

These past few weeks have made me more steadfast than ever that we won't win this with guns. Or an arsenal. I fault no one for wanting one. For needing an extra sense of security. I believe they can be useful. Should our country divulge into complete civil unrest, more useful than we ever could have imagined. But for the fight—the day in and day out revolutionary fight—no. What keeps them in places in power—what keeps them commanding such large groups of young men and women who don't question the asinine orders or culture of harming the most vulnerable in society in the name of "protection"—is knowledge. It's the written word and their inability to comprehend it. To me, that is the real weapon. That is the nuclear bomb.

You know as well as I do from your place in academia that we live in a country that relishes in the idea of the anti-intellectual. "Not everyone need be educated" and "tons of millionaires didn't go to college" are quips I hear from my home in the South constantly. I hear it from those fighting to make their way in a capitalistic world who did not receive a traditional education and feel "less than," trying to hide behind the rhetoric of "not needing" that to fill (what they believe) to be a deficit. Capitalism has robbed us of the core purpose of knowledge. Here we are told that education is only as good as the money it can make you. There is no need to know a thing if it cannot put wealth in your pockets or elevate your status. And for this our country is dying. We must confront this lie. This is more dangerous than any gun we think we need.

The thought of "not needing" education is perpetuated by the rich. The same people who "pay" for their children to be admitted into prestigious colleges although they have billions themselves. Whose wayward children, after proving unable to be taught, are used to connect with other wealthy families and "marry" wealth. Like voting, if education didn't matter, why would they care for their own children to have it? Why would they make college so expensive? Withhold funding for public schools? Why would Betsy DeVos exist? Because they know it's a weapon too. The ability to critically think and detect lies from truths with verifiable sources will be the end of them.

We know they know it because of our military. American Armed forces recruits go and find young people who can't find a path and teach them what they want them to know. They offer them housing. Food. Healthcare. The state becomes their caretakers in a world where they can otherwise not thrive because of their socio-economic status and just like we all do with our parents, they adopt the beliefs of the state and that flows down to their non-duty families. Their friends. Their communities. Even those that don't become servicemen but are from the same cloth follow closely behind. America promised folks life, liberty, and the pursuit of happiness. In a capitalistic society that means money. Servicemen are shown a path where—if they just do what they are told—they can be comfortable. Why would they stray from that? Why would they question any other way? They had certainly never seen anything else. There was no access to other lifestyles, or ways of being, or cultures. Harvard doesn't recruit. The Army does. About fourteen thousand students enter the Ivy Leagues each year. One hundred and eighty thousand join the military. Those numbers are telling. We have successfully made learning inaccessible. A privilege. Fighting, being a Ward of the Country, is open to anyone.

We did not go to Ivy League schools. At least I didn't. After we left Florida State you did just that. I remember watching you with such reverence. I wondered how you had done it. Even with a decent education, that "level" felt so far away. I will contend for the rest of my life that our undergraduate years were

Tallahassee's prime. Between FAMU and FSU, the city birthed some of the most brilliant minds the world has had to contend with to date. Non-recruited minds from Miami Dade County and Chicago and Virginia and tiny beach towns in Florida. Schools weren't checking for us. But for one reason or another, we were checking for school. We had all certainly been taught that you "couldn't get a job without a degree." Which, at the time, was true. Now, we have found that capitalism has moved the goal post yet again. To get a high-paying job out of under-grad, you need a post-secondary degree. It is making folks discredit education, forego spending money to receive a piece of paper that won't make them money. But that should have never been the point. It wasn't education's original intent.

Today, reading is reserved for "smart" people. It's an "elitist" practice—the biggest con this country's cult of ignorance has allowed the populous to believe. Folks turn to movies and TV now. A bunch of people want to *be* on TV and in movies as a way to deliver messages and have voice in our country, never realizing that to do so still requires the written word. Pages and pages every week. Every project. Someone is still writing them. Someone is still responsible for those words. That's why I am here. That's where I feel we win this fight. It's not as "heroic" as the guns-blazing, "come one step closer to this porch and I'll shoot you" scenes we have played in our heads for so long. But to me, it is far more impactful. When DuBois and Baldwin were at the zenith of their careers, there was no Netflix. No smart phone. No distractions. Those books—the written word—were how information was disseminated. Those words could travel from Louisiana to Los Angeles and back to

Harlem and be discussed almost everywhere they touched. Now they spread through cable lines and satellites. And it's instant. We've never been up against such a cult of ignorance. We've never had to fight so many who have been taught to deprive themselves of the very information they need to make more sound decisions. We've also never had so many avenues to present information. And never this fast.

For years you've tried to get us all to see that divesting from the police was the only way. I've seen you speak about it. Heard you. I've read papers about it and seen the books written about the topic sparsely discussed. I am sad to admit that I never paid attention. It didn't seem plausible to me at first glance and even I, an avid reader and writer and academic, did not look more into it because it wasn't presented easily enough. How much more easily must the average American need something to be presented? It is not that those works were in vain. Quite the contrary. When the video of George Floyd was released and the battle cry of "Defund the Police" came to the forefront you all were ready. The facts were there. The statistics were there. The narrative was there. Everyone was willing to jump on board, and quickly, because the plan was in motion. It just needed people.

It was that video that got the people. It was watching Tamika not mince words behind that podium. It was watching Kimberly's eloquent rage as she deadpanned into the camera that the social contract was broken. It was the footage of that car on Fairfax. It was the images of a statue of Robert E. Lee now tagged and lit with the faces of those we lost. The on-the-ground coverage from protests. Instagram Lives. The spoken word pieces. The children. The tears. So few can pick up a book or a novel anymore and feel the rush of human emotions we felt when Sula cuts her finger—an attempt at intimidation by showing if she is crazy enough to hurt herself, what more would she do to those that would try to annihilate her. Asking someone to read Morrison or Newton or even one of your own papers to get a grasp of what is going on and develop a plan of action is not only antiquated but out of touch. Our people have been robbed of the *desire* for knowledge for so long that all they want is a solution for their problem, delivered in its most digestible form. Making information available is no longer a plausible strategy any more than getting a shotgun is, thinking we can protect our property when drones exist.

This is where I now feel most aligned. I'm the recruiter that never came to our towns or for our folks. Get the information to the people visually, with a spoonful of sugar. When it inspires them to action, I pass them off to you.

Self-awareness is a strong suit. I know my own fear of safety for my son and self-preservation plays into this too. Maybe that's why I've thought about this so much. I'm also grounded enough (maybe old-fashioned enough) to know that even the biggest blockbuster or widely-watched TV show could never replace on-the-ground organizing. Grassroots birthed me. It taught me how to sit in someone's living room and hear them. To not prescribe my answer to their problem but rather allow them to tell me what they want the answer to their problem to be—even if I disagree—and help them devise the plan to get it. To walk away from a community wishing they had pushed for more equity, for better treatment, but resting confident in knowing we gave them the tools for that—the resources and knowledge—should they ever want something more. To devise a plan. To disrupt. To fight. TV could never do that.

But what we can do (what *I* can do) is show them what the fight can look like. Inspire them to want to fight. I can show them what the world could be. Inspire them to create that. Show them how they are being conned. What information is being hidden. How history has repeated itself. I can do that. Then they can call Tamika and Stephen Green and Linda and Patrisse and Alberto and all the bodies on the ground, in the community, doing the day in and day out work and say "I want to change it too." Then those people will say, "Fantastic. Now that you are here, here is a work by our esteemed colleague Chaz. Read it to learn the ins and outs of what we fight for." It all works in tandem.

None of it includes guns. It can't. There's too much groundwork and organizing that needs to be covered first. Folks don't even know who the enemy is.

As controversial as the piece is, I still love Hamilton, for every artistic reason a person can muster. While the tales of the Revolution are not quite our own, and in some ways are the worst of our stories, there are lessons there for us. America's founding fathers—and I am careful to say America's and not ours because they are not ours nor will they ever be—did not win the war because everyone had a gun. Because they shot back. They killed thousands of Brits, and thousands more came back with newer guns. Bigger guns. More ammo. Canons. There was no solace in knowing "at least I killed one Redcoat." There was terror in knowing no matter how many they killed more would come. The battle turned with strategy. It turned with a plan that only the scrappy, the desperate, the hell-bent-on-freedom could enact. They stole cannons. They provoked national outrage to keep their own resources pouring in. They attacked covertly, swiftly, and with precision. They outlasted the enemy until the enemy was in their territory and imploded. They waved their flags. They'd had enough. *Make it impossible to justify the cost of the fight.*

Chaz, I know it sounds crazy to believe that America would ever relent when they gain cheap labor and make each other billions. But history has shown the tide can change. This summer, this moment, is showing us that it can change. Enough disruption can tear it down. Public outrage because of our treatment in defense of ourselves bolsters our resources; we've seen it this summer. It gets us in more homes. It pushes our stories in front of more people. I am not of the mind that we don't defend ourselves. I am not Martin. If someone hits you, knock their fucking head off. There is no such thing as "going high" when a system will only ever see you as low. But there is also no such thing as matching firepower in our situation. Sixty years ago, maybe. Not today.

Too much has changed. But also, so little has. Herschel is us. The American Revolution is now. Strategy won all those wars. Innovation. We can do that, and more humanely.

A lot of people are going to die. A lot already have. It keeps me up at night. I look at my son and wonder if one day...I can't even type it. I think it all the time, but I can't allow the words to roll off of my tongue. I wonder. In that wondering I know beyond a shadow of a doubt that I would kill for him. If I saw a knee on his neck or a so-called neighborhood patrol harassing him and I had a weapon I would, without hesitation, defend my son. I also know that they could and likely would kill us both. I don't fear my own death. I didn't save my baby. The "satisfaction" of knowing I went out with a fight would not be there. He would be gone. That would be all that mattered.

What can we do to save our kids? It's not as bald as a pistol in our pocket and let the chips fall where they may. It's not as simple as I once thought it to be—infiltrate from within does not work. It's something new. Something we have never done. But something that has surely been done already, at some point in history.

I hope you have the answers.

—V

PS: I ordered the books.

* * *

DEAR CHAZ,

This will be short. We've been reading, and corresponding. We've been talking and I've been mulling over. I only have thoughts, not answers. It seems the same for you. I'm feeling hopeless now. Like nothing will ever work. I feel ashamed for my hopelessness. I'm more quiet than usual, except to you. A few others. I'm savoring every moment of my son's happiness. His jumping on the couch or his dreams of growing up to be a shark. This world is going to kick his ass and make it her duty to rob him of all his exuberance and I'm offering my body as a living sacrifice to stave that off as long as I can.

As you can imagine, I'm pretty beaten up. You are a parent. You are too.

I don't think it will ever be in me to want to "get someone because they tried to get me." It's just not who I am. I never want revenge or retribution or for others to feel the pain I feel. Only for them to see it—to see me or the person they've hurt—and care. To feel remorse and know they were wrong and change. I still think it possible for a lot of white folks in the country. Bur far less than I did even a day ago.

I want to believe that arming ourselves is the answer. Or even part of the answer. I would love to be as ideological as I was in my youth. I want to think that we can burn this entire system down and replace it with something better and more equitable. But humans. We cannot legislate or make illegal the human desire for power. It will rise again as it always does. The fight will change and my most sincere hope is that, by some strange and lucky chance should I live to see the day this version of America is transformed into the mockup of my college mind, I'm not so cynical that I don't believe we won. That anyone can ever win. I've looked at every country that has bits and pieces of the "model" nation I wish for. Oppression is there. Someone, some group, is being shat on somewhere because of one or several men's need to rule. Even where they claim "power to the people" there is a well-known overlord. Can we win? What is winning?

I'm beaten up.

The colors of this world would be less vibrant, smells less intense, and tastes dull without my child. I don't know what I was doing before he got here. I am still very much my own person; my identity is not merely his mother. But I would be remiss to say that he didn't force me to figure out who I was or give me the bravery to change that perception when necessary so as to be the best me I could be to be the best mother to him. His life did that for mine. He has been my gift. And my death. George Floyd calling for his mother has beaten me up. Oh, if my baby called for me and I couldn't pull a knee off of his neck. Oh, if he called for me I would use whatever I had to physically stop that officer from touching my boy. Oh, what would I do if they killed me on the spot and in my last breath I did not know if I had saved my son? What could I do if I didn't? What could he do if I did? What kind of life is any of this, Chaz?

The ebbs and flows of these emotions are hard. Oscillating between terror and trying to organize to despair is more than our nervous systems are designed to handle, I think. At this point, if anyone set it all on fire, I would not fight them. Or tell them it was futile. But like the car on Fairfax I would only watch it from the balcony and try to keep the ash from getting in my baby's eyes. I feel as though I have so little to give the movement because of my devotion to my son, and so little to give my son for the same reason. Tamika gives me hope. She riles me up. She inspires me. But I stay on that balcony. There I write furiously *(why do I write like I'm running out of time)* and pray that it will be something. That somehow it will inspire a new way to think about sinking ships and self-defense and disruption and life and humanity and people.

That at the very least someone will see someone on TV and relate to how much we all love our goddamn kids and want them alive.

But until they see us, until I can figure out how to see myself in this moment, I am so grateful that you see me. That you organize my heart. You allow me to arrive at conclusions you disagree with but give me the tools to change my mind later and fight for more. You give me the space I don't give myself: the space to fight terrified.

I love you. Send my love to B + F.

—*V*

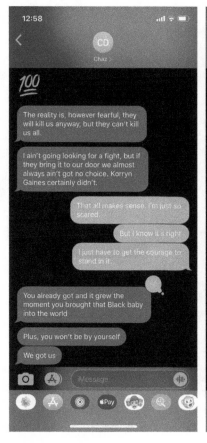

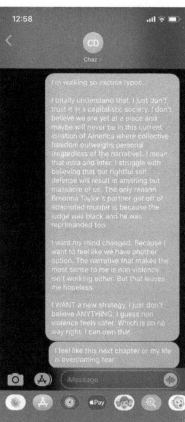

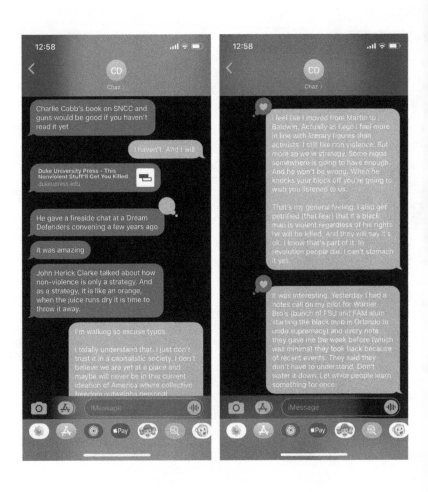

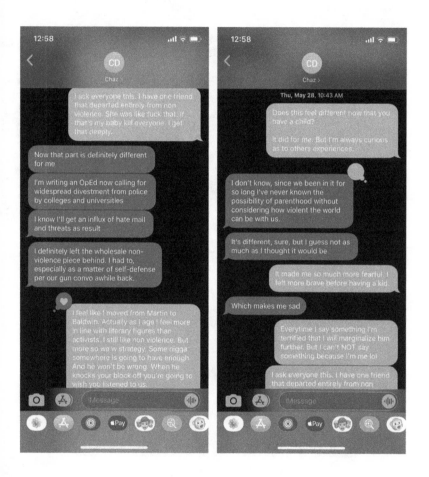

VANESSA BADEN KELLY

ABOUT THE AUTHOR

Vanessa Baden Kelly is an Emmy winning actress, Emmy nominated writer, and producer. She began her career as a child, starring on Nickelodeon's *Gullah Gullah Island* and *Kenan and Kel*. After departing entertainment, she began organizing in college, co-founding the Student Coalition for Justice (later the base for the Dream Defenders) and continued working in the field. To date, she has led campaigns for The Trayvon Martin Foundation, Community Coalition South LA, and various political campaigns including Obama for America '08 and the Ndoum Presidential Campaign in Accra, Ghana. Additionally, she is an Ambassador for the RuJohn Foundation. Upon her return to Hollywood, Vanessa has become a successful television writer and producer, writing for shows such as TNT's *Animal Kingdom* and Mindy Kaling's HBO Max series *The Sex Lives of College Girls*. Vanessa originated the role of Journee as writer/star of the Issa Rae digital series *Giants*, where she is four times Emmy-nominated and one time Emmy-winning for Best Actress in a Digital Drama. Vanessa is mother to a human son, Ryder, and a dog son named Dude.

RECENT AND FORTHCOMING BOOKS FROM THREE ROOMS PRESS

Three Rooms Press | New York, NY | Current Catalog: www.threeroomspress.com
Three Rooms Press books are distributed worldwide by PGW/Ingram: www.pgw.com